CHEMICAL NIGHTMARE

"It doesn't happen just in the United States. It can happen here — right in our own backyard."
— *Hedy Gervais, a mother of two children, who formerly lived across from the Upper Ottawa Street landfill in Hamilton, Ontario.*

CHEMICAL NIGHTMARE

The Unnecessary Legacy of Toxic Wastes

by John Jackson, Phil Weller, & the Waterloo Public Interest Research Group

between the lines

© 1982 The Waterloo Public Interest Research Group

Published by:	Between The Lines 427 Bloor St. W. Toronto, Ontario, Canada
Typeset by:	Dumont Press Graphix 97 Victoria St. N. Kitchener, Ontario, Canada
Printed by:	The Alger Press Limited Oshawa, Ontario, Canada
Cover photo:	© 1975 by Doug Wicken
Song on page 65:	© 1981 by Dennis O'Toole

*Between The Lines receives financial assistance
from the Ontario Arts Council.*

Canadian Cataloguing in Publication Data

Jackson, John.
  Chemical nightmare

ISBN 0-919946-26-7 (bound). — ISBN 0-919946-27-5

1. Factory and trade waste — Environmental aspects.
2. Pollution — Environmental aspects. 3. Waste disposal
in the ground. I. Weller, Phil, 1956- II. Waterloo Public
Interest Research Group. III. Title.

TD897.J33   363.7'384   C83-098036-9

TABLE OF CONTENTS

Some of the terms used in this book are explained in the
Glossary on page 114.

PREFACE

COLOUR SLIDES OF NEATLY PILED 55-gallon drums, sparkling equipment, and laboratories shine in front of our eyes as we sit in the darkened meeting room beside the Tricil liquid waste disposal facility near Sarnia. After this visual presentation by the plant manager and the company salesman, we put on hard hats and safety glasses for our tour of the incinerator and landfill. We stare into the glowing inferno of the furnace into which liquid wastes are injected and burned. Meters and dials surround the furnace. We walk among pipes and tanks where wastes are separated and mixed. A 225-foot stack towers above us. It being a dull, drizzly day, our guide chooses not to take us back to see the open lagoon and the landfill where a truck is now backed up dumping wastes. "The road is too muddy," he says. We leave suitably impressed by our guided tour, assured that all is well at this waste disposal facility.

We drive past the bush separating the Tricil operation from the surrounding farms of Lambton County. The evening is spent at a nearby farmhouse sitting around the kitchen table, chatting with local residents. For five hours they express the frustration that has resulted from their decade of experiences with Tricil and the Ontario Ministry of the Environment — unanswered questions, spills, ruined crops, smells.

As we go out to our car to leave, we stand in the farm lane and stare at the incinerator stack clearly visible in the black night sky, a heavy grey plume of emissions flowing from it. Watching the stack, we wonder how often those who make the decisions about the handling of hazardous wastes have sat in the kitchens of neighbours to a waste facility and chatted long into the evening.

In this book, we share with you the insights about the hazardous wastes problem that we have gained during the past year of research and of talking with those concerned about and experienced with this problem. We describe the extent of the problem and

7

the ways in which business, government, and citizens are dealing with it.

Although we focus on Ontario, the emphasis is not on legislation and institutions specific to that province. Instead, we have used the detailed example of Ontario to show the different kinds of responses to the hazardous wastes issue. The lessons of Ontario are relevant elsewhere. In an appendix, the dimensions of the hazardous waste problem and government plans for dealing with that problem in each part of Canada are summarized.

We have spent considerable time sitting in kitchens and living rooms across southern Ontario talking with those whose communities have unexpectedly been confronted by the threat of hazardous wastes. These people have shared with us their invaluable knowledge and penetrating understanding of the management of hazardous wastes. We have conducted interviews with the following members of these groups: Shiela May and Allan Freeman of the Binbrook Anti-Dump Committee, Diane Jacobs, Mike Newnham and Lillian Tomen of Citizens Rebelling Against Waste, Hedy Gervais of the Upper Ottawa Street Citizens Group, Elaine Fritz, Fran Sainsbury, and Fran Sutton of the Concerned Citizens of Whitchurch-Stouffville, Phil Hinman and the board of directors of the Haldimand-Norfolk Organization for a Pure Environment, Sherry Morrison and several members of the Lambton Anti-Pollution Association, Margherita Howe of Operation Clean Niagara, and Moni Campbell of Pollution Probe. Throughout every stage of the research and writing of this book, this collection of Ontario citizens' groups has offered information, encouragement, and inspiration.

Important assistance has been received from several government employees. Boris Boyko, Paul Isles, and Carol Olchowsky of Ontario's Ministry of the Environment gave us lengthy interviews. Anne Koven of the Ministry of Health's Upper Ottawa Street Landfill Site Study shared with us her experiences in investigating the problems at the Hamilton landfill. Members of Environment Canada and the Ontario Waste Management Corporation made government reports available to us; Jeanne Jabanoski, the information director for the Ontario region of Environment Canada, was particularly helpful.

Industry publications have provided us with much significant information. Interviews with Jim Stewart of Chemical and Petro Waste Disposal Limited and Steen Klint and Eric Hunter of Tricil Limited made important contributions to our understanding of the problem.

The proposal for this book emerged from an annual gathering of Ontario Public Interest Research Groups (PIRGs) in Peterborough during the summer of 1981. PIRGs (student funded and directed research and educational organizations) had previously undertaken research on hazardous waste management and it was felt that an easily read resource was needed to facilitate informed public discussion of this important issue. The board and staff of the Waterloo Public Interest Research Group have at all times offered support, ideas and assistance as have members of other Ontario PIRGs. Donna Elliot of Hamilton has been notable among these. A grant from Employment and Immigration Canada to OPIRG -Windsor contributed to the salary of one of the authors of this book.

Finally, we thank Lois Berry, Anne Koven, Diane Jacobs, Ann Pinnegar, Fran Sainsbury, Doug Saunders and Lillian Tomen who read the manuscript and made corrections and suggestions which have greatly improved its content. Members of the publishing collective Between The Lines have also given us important editorial comments.

This book was only possible because of those people who shared their experiences and knowledge with us. They did so because of their belief that a more informed public will result in action being taken to deal with this serious problem. We hope that this book will make a contribution to improved public understanding and the eventual elimination of the dangers caused by hazardous wastes.

John Jackson
Phil Weller
December 1982

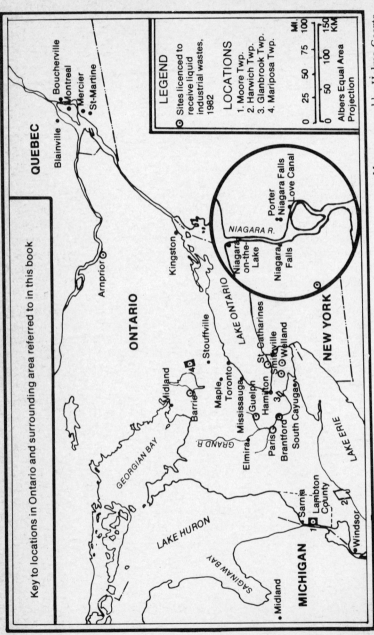

Key to locations in Ontario and surrounding area referred to in this book

LEGEND

⊙ Sites licenced to
receive liquid
industrial wastes,
1982

LOCATIONS
1. Moore Twp.
2. Harwich Twp.
3. Glanbrook Twp.
4. Mariposa Twp.

Albers Equal Area
Projection

QUEBEC

Boucherville
Montreal
Mercier
St-Martine
Blainville

Arnprior

ONTARIO

Kingston

NIAGARA R.

Niagara-
on-the-
Lake

Niagara
Falls

Porter
Niagara Falls
Love Canal

NEW YORK

Midland
Barrie
Maple
Stouffville
Toronto
Mississauga
Guelph
Elmira
Hamilton
Paris
Brantford
South Cayuga
St. Catharines
Smithville
Welland

LAKE ONTARIO

LAKE ERIE

GRAND R.

GEORGIAN BAY

LAKE HURON

Sarnia
Lambton County
Windsor

MICHIGAN

Midland

SAGINAW BAY

Map prepared by Helma Geerts

INTRODUCTION

"THE CATTLE STARTED getting sick and they started dying," reported Leander Martin, a Mennonite farmer who lives on a 173-acre farm near Elmira, Ontario.[1] Their illnesses, 15 deaths, and tainted milk were caused by drinking from the creek that wanders across his farm — a creek contaminated by toxic wastes from a nearby chemical company. In the hopes of avoiding further problems, Leander Martin fenced off the creek so his cattle could not drink from it; this meant abandoning 20 acres of his property.

For several decades, Uniroyal Ltd. used this creek as a convenient dump to wash away its hazardous wastes. To make matters worse, in 1969 the company buried millions of gallons of chemical wastes in two pits at its Elmira chemical plant. Included in these wastes was trichlorophenol, often used in manufacturing herbicides. Although not produced intentionally, inevitably present with trichlorophenol are dioxins, one of which, TCDD, is commonly referred to by scientists as the most poisonous chemical ever produced. In minute quantities, this dioxin produces birth defects and cancers. Wastes from these pits have been found to be leaking toward the creek.

Tests in the early 1980's by the Ontario Ministry of the Environment found increased contamination in the creek. This creek empties into the Grand River, which provides water for several southern Ontario communities. A surface water specialist with the Ministry of the Environment concluded, "The things we are finding [in the water], we don't know the significance of."[2]

* * *

IN AN AREA known as Quebec's vegetable garden and as one of the province's main sources of milk, 8,000 people were told by the provincial government in 1982 not to drink from their wells because of chemical contamination from a nearby waste disposal site.[3]

11

Between 1968 and 1973, millions of gallons of liquid industrial wastes were poured into an old gravel pit just outside of Mercier, a town 12 miles southwest of Montreal. Chemical pollution from the site has been spreading underground. By 1982, groundwater underneath 12 square miles of farmland had been permanently contaminated; chemical levels in the water were found to be 1000 times higher than allowed by federal government drinking water standards. No one knows how much further this contamination will go.

All residents within one mile south of the lagoon were ordered not to drink from their wells. Quebec's Environment Ministry told vegetable growers within that same area not to use the water for the irrigation of their rich, black soils. St-Martine's main industry, a Green Giant food processing plant employing 600 people, now has its water supply threatened.

Despite its efforts to stop the spread of contamination, the Quebec government fears that an ever-expanding section of this water supply, one of Quebec's largest reserves of underground fresh water, is being permanently poisoned.

* * *

DURING THE MID-1970's, the stack of a liquid waste incinerator on the Hamilton beach front belched heavy smoke, saturating the air with foul smells and ash. Neighbours complained about the smells; they experienced respiratory problems and eye irritations that they suspected were caused by these emissions. The quantities of wastes burnt frequently exceeded the amount permitted by the company's licence. A foreman at the site said, "That stuff would stink like rotten eggs."[4]

Among the wastes burnt at the site were radioactive materials and polychlorinated biphenyls (PCBs), formerly a common component of electrical transformers.[5] The federal government considers PCBs to be so dangerous that it has banned their use in new equipment. The substance is an almost indestructible cancer-causing agent and exposure to it can also produce acne-like skin eruptions, still births, and infant deformities.

As a result of persistent public pressure, the liquid waste incinerator was closed in 1977.

* * *

IN THE SUMMER OF 1981, a black gooey tar oozed out of the ground in a suburban Sarnia schoolyard.[6] Tests showed that the sticky substance contained styrene, benzene, and polyethylbenzene, each

of which is known to cause skin problems and is suspected of causing cancers. A quarter of the schoolyard was fenced off and the
wastes were dug up.

Thirty years earlier, Dow Chemical Ltd. had used this spot as a
catch basin for its chemical wastes. These chemicals, long forgotten
and unrecorded, have begun to return to the surface to haunt the
people that live in the Twin Lakes housing development. No one
knows how much further these wastes stretch out under the subdivision. It is suspected that the weight of the buildings is causing
the chemical wastes to be pushed up. The industrial abatement
officer in the Sarnia branch of the Ontario Ministry of the Environment said that if construction continues they may have hazardous
wastes "popping to the surface all over the place".[7]

* * *

AT A LIQUID waste incinerator in Michigan, on January 13, 1982, a
23-year-old worker was overcome by deadly fumes. He had been
transferring liquid wastes from a tanker truck into a holding tank
when chemical reactions caused the release of hydrogen sulphide
gas. An older worker rushed to his aid, but he too was instantly
overcome by the fumes. Both were killed.

A spokesperson for the Detroit Firefighters Union reported, "In
large amounts you can't smell it [hydrogen sulphide gas] because
the gas immediately destroys your sense of smell. You die as a
result of your lungs burning out from the acid that is created in
your system."[8]

Fearing contamination from the fumes that saturated the dead
workers' bodies, rescue workers had to keep their distance. The
bodies were left for more than eight hours before being carried off
in military plastic body bags. Fifty other people, including 19 rescue workers, suffered ill effects from the gas.

Neighbours had been complaining for a long time about conditions at the liquid waste incinerator. As a result of investigations
after the deaths of the two workers, the Environmental Protection
Agency required more stringent controls at the facility. Two
months later, the owners deserted the waste disposal operation.
They abandoned large volumes of hazardous wastes, leaving them
sitting in tanks and pits at the site.

* * *

EXAMPLES SUCH AS THESE of the inadequate handling of hazardous wastes can be found all across North America. People are
becoming more aware of the long-term devastating consequences

of this mismanagement. This book explores the ways in which corporations, governments and the public have been dealing with the hazardous wastes issue in Ontario.

Our living and working environments are being contaminated from many sources, resulting in a wide range of different problems. Each of these seemingly disparate problems has direct links to the others. Each is the unplanned and unwanted by-product of this chemical society. Although the possible contaminants that affect us are many, our interest usually focuses upon one of these problems — the problem that most directly affects our own lives. But as Bob Sass and Richard Butler, both of Saskatchewan's Department of Labour, have said,

> ... how many of us grasp the significance of the *cumulative* effect of all these apparently unrelated events? How many of us see them as part of an ongoing trend — the gradual but unrelenting poisoning of our country?[9]

Residents of Harwich Township in southwestern Ontario have fought for several years to protect themselves against the perils of a liquid waste dump in their community. After a long battle punctuated by both temporary victories and defeats, they forced the government to ban the dumping of liquid industrial wastes at the site in late 1981. They remained worried, however, about the effects of the tons of hazardous wastes that were dumped before anyone in the community was aware of what was happening.

Their concern began over toxic wastes, and there the focus remained. But as they explored their situation, they gained a new understanding of people worried about other issues, and recognized the links between those problems and their own.

They became sympathetic with the people in northern Ontario where the government has suggested disposing of radioactive wastes by burying them in deep wells in the Canadian Shield. They also realized their connection with people who work in factories. The toxic substances that were shipped to Harwich are handled every day by working people as part of their regular jobs. Frequently, these workers come even more directly into contact with these substances, and often in greater concentrations.

Harwich residents asked questions about the items consumed in this society — the by-products of which became the wastes poured into the Harwich landfill. Do these toxic by-products mean that there are also toxic substances in the items themselves? How safe are the foods and the materials produced? They realized that the people who use these products come into contact with toxic

photo: Mark Trusz

Rear view of Uniroyal plant in Elmira, Ontario, with the Canagagigue Creek in the foreground.

materials either by eating them, by inhaling their fumes, or by touching them.

In these ways, what at first seemed to be a narrow concern about a toxic waste dump became recognized as having much in common with the concerns of numerous other people. Each problem is directly linked to a particular hazardous substance that contaminates the environment. But those worried about these issues now realize that the commonality goes much further.

Since 1971, Bob McArthur has worked in the salt mines in Windsor, Ontario. Six days a week he goes 1000 feet below the surface to work in the forty-foot wide and twenty-foot high caverns that stretch out from the Detroit River. When freshly cut, the walls sparkle and shine with the white of the salt. But they are quickly blackened by the exhaust from diesel equipment used to carry rock salt around in this underground city. Needless to say, those who work below the surface breathe air heavy with diesel emissions, air that contains benzo-a-pyrene, a known cause of cancer.

Bob McArthur and his fellow workers have spent several years trying to persuade the company to take corrective action and the Ontario Ministry of Labour to force the company to take measures to protect workers' health. After a long struggle, some important improvements have been made.

As Bob McArthur heard about the experiences of people in Harwich, he realized that these people were encountering the same kinds of problems as he and his co-workers. This is what he had to say about it:

> The issue they were dealing with was different, but the players are the same.
>
> They were just average, ordinary people trying to protect themselves against a highly toxic substance, something that could ruin their land and their livelihood, their health and their children's health. Those things are common not only to their issue, but to the occupational health issue, the environmental issues, the nuclear issue, or any of those things.
>
> But they ended up finding they had to rely upon themselves, because they couldn't count on their government and they couldn't count on the company who was the polluter. They were encountering the same forces as we did in the salt mine.[10]

Although this book focuses on the ways in which corporations, governments, and citizens have been dealing with the problem of hazardous wastes, its actual scope is much broader. As the salt miners in Windsor and the people of Harwich have discovered, they are all encountering the same forces. Therefore, the hazardous wastes problem can be seen as a case study; through a careful analysis of it, we draw closer to understanding many other issues in this chemical society.

This book begins by briefly outlining the extent and the nature of the hazardous wastes problem. We then explore how the waste management industry and Ontario's provincial government have been handling the situation. One of the most controversial aspects of this problem is the search for new disposal facilities and the public's repeated rejections of those new proposals. The ways in which this process has become bogged down are examined. Finally, we describe existing waste management strategies that could dramatically reduce the problems being created by hazardous wastes.

CHAPTER ONE
THE HAZARDOUS WASTES PROBLEM

UNRECORDED QUANTITIES of hazardous industrial wastes have been disposed of by unknowing, inexperienced, and unconcerned companies. These wastes are welling up to pose serious dangers in many communities. In the coming years, as more past errors surface, the number of contamination problems can be expected to increase dramatically.

Almost 800 dump sites previously unknown to the Ontario government were discovered in a survey carried out during the summer of 1979. The research team estimated that between 2000 and 3000 more unrecorded sites may exist in southern Ontario.[1] Although many of these sites do not pose hazards to human health or the environment, others do.

In 1979, a consultant for the United States Environmental Protection Agency estimated that there were as many as 50,000 chemical dumps in the United States; he suspected that between 1200 and 2000 of these posed significant dangers.[2]

Even after these far-reaching government searches, two mysteries remain: 1) how many former dumps still have not been found? and 2) what hazardous chemicals are in the sites already located?

The Nature of the Problem

UNFORTUNATELY, THE PROBLEMS of waste management are not just creatures of the past. "Hazardous wastes are an inevitable, though undesirable, by-product of modern life," according to the Chemical Manufacturers' Association.[3] Most corporate managers would agree that the welfare of society depends upon the constant expansion of production. By implication, this means there will also be a constant expansion of wastes.

Therefore, even though government, business, and scientists realize the extreme seriousness of the contamination that results from improper waste disposal, the production of hazardous wastes continues to expand. As Richard Brownstein, author of a chapter in the book, *Who's Poisoning America?* pointed out:

> When the federal emergency was declared there in 1978, Love Canal contained a little more than 43 million pounds of hazardous wastes, deposited during a decade by Hooker Chemical Company. In 1980 alone, America produced 125 billion pounds of hazardous wastes, or enough to fill approximately 3,000 Love Canals.[4]

The Canadian federal government estimated in 1982 that at least 3.2 million tonnes of hazardous wastes are generated in Canada each year.[5]

Not only are the quantities of wastes increasing, but also the types of wastes generated are becoming more numerous and knowledge of their impacts harder to grasp. Since the 1940's, manufacturing processes have rapidly become more dependent upon newly created chemicals. Fifty-five thousand different chemicals are now in industrial use in North America,[6] and more than 700 new chemicals are introduced into industry each year.[7] The widely respected expert on chemical pollutants, Dr. Samuel Epstein, has pointed out that many of these chemicals are "not just familiar ones, but exotic ones which have never previously existed on earth and to which no living thing has previously had to adapt."[8]

Those who live next door to the discarded wastes of this chemical production risk such unknown hazards. But it is not only the nearby residents who are affected. Workers in waste disposal operations are often the forgotten victims of the improper handling of hazardous wastes, suffering injuries and sometimes death in disposal accidents. But the untold toll is of those who have developed cancers or other disabling diseases because of contact with toxic substances at work. Clean-ups of old toxic waste dumps can pose considerable hazards to workers. In such a situation, there is substantial potential for explosions and sudden release of poisonous fumes from unknown mixtures of chemicals.

Unexpected exposure to these wastes also occurs as a result of spills during the transportation of hazardous materials. In the two years after the 1979 Mississauga train derailment, which entailed the evacuation of 240,000 people, there were 106 spills of dangerous goods in Canada involving rail transportation.[9] Transport Canada recorded 175 spills of dangerous goods from trucks during 1980 and 1981. But the Transport of Dangerous Goods Branch said that "the statistics for transport accident by road are grossly underestimated."[10] Canadian government statistics do not distinguish between spills involving wastes and other hazardous materials.

The overwhelming majority of spills of dangerous wastes do not occur while the waste is actually on the rails or on the road. A 1980 study carried out for the government of Alberta estimated that over 96 percent of these accidents occur during loading and unloading.[11]

Leaking toxic chemical dumps, improperly operated waste incinerators, and chemical waste spills can each spread their dangers far beyond their immediate vicinities. Once chemicals enter a drainage basin, the flow of water carries them across a considerable amount of territory throughout which their effects will be felt. If they are washed into a creek, they could contaminate the drinking water of people and animals or the irrigation waters for crops and gardens. The creek inevitably flows into a river and passes cities and towns. If it is in southern Ontario, the river will empty into one of the Great Lakes and be carried eventually to the Atlantic Ocean. Along the route, these waste-laden waters will be used by an ever-expanding number of people, animals, and vegetation for their nutrition.

Thus, improper dumping affects not only those in the immediate vicinity of the contamination but also a considerably larger part of the population.

Dilution of chemicals by mixing them with greater and greater quantities of water does not remove their hazards. The real effect of dilution is to disperse toxic wastes throughout the environment, spreading their potential hazards. In their 1979 report to the Canadian Environmental Advisory Council, Dr. Ross Hall, a biochemist, and Dr. Donald Chant, a zoologist, concluded:

> Use, waste, and ultimate discard of chemicals in all forms pervade the environment in massive and insidious ways. Their rapid dispersion and invasive power make it impossible to localize their effects. Consequently, the whole environment, including humans, is being contaminated in a sea of chemicals. [12]

The Great Lakes have become a catchbasin for many of these chemicals. Out of 400 chemicals that have been found in the Great Lakes, the International Joint Commission has identified at least 380 as having potentially harmful effects on human life.[13] A major addition to this chemical brew comes from the ravaged Niagara River into which large volumes of industrial waste are discharged each day and into which chemical-bearing leachate seeps from many of the 200 hazardous waste dumps sown along its shores. Dow Chemical Co. in Midland, Michigan, has long been another substantial source of contaminants in the Great Lakes. This company, a major producer of pesticides and chemicals, has polluted

Saginaw Bay with dioxin, PCBs, DDT, and other known toxic substances, giving the bay the distinction, according to the International Joint Commission, of being one of the most polluted areas in
the Great Lakes.[14] Its waters go into Lake Huron and flow through
the rest of the Great Lakes system, multiplying the pollution
already caused by hazardous wastes discharged from countless
other sources.

The impacts of the contamination of the Great Lakes catchbasin
have been dramatic. In 1982, traces of the deadliest known poison,
dioxin, were found in a human body in Kingston, the first detection
of this lethal substance in a person in North America, except among
veterans of the Vietnam war.[15] The breast milk of mothers living in
southern Ontario contains a number of chemical contaminants,
including PCBs.[16] Health and Welfare Canada surveys during the
late 1970's found contamination levels in mothers' milk well above
the acceptable daily intake for infants. Some kinds of fish have been
declared by Ontario's Ministry of the Environment as unsafe for
human consumption because of the presence of toxic chemicals
absorbed into their flesh. The Great Lakes region is not the only
area in which this process of destruction is happening. Water quality is deteriorating all across Canada.

Not all industrial wastes are hazardous. Governments usually
state that 10 per cent of these wastes are hazardous, but this is only
an estimate. While it is difficult to actually determine whether a
waste substance is damaging to the environment or human health,
if it has one of the following characteristics it is classified as
hazardous: ignitability at a relatively low temperature, corrosivity
(highly acidic or alkaline), reactivity (explodes or generates gases
or fumes), toxicity (produces acute or chronic health effects on people or animals or affects the growth of plants), radioactivity, infec-
tiousness, carcinogenicity (causes cancers), mutagenicity (damages
the genes thus affecting future generations of humans, animals or
plants) or teratogenicity (causes birth defects). Yet it is often not
possible to determine whether a waste is hazardous simply by running down this list. Three questions of an often controversial
nature must be asked: 1) does the substance have the character-
istic? 2) what degree of the hazard is acceptable? and, 3) who will
decide this?

The ability to produce new chemicals has far outstripped our
society's scientific ability to test them. It is extremely difficult to
determine the long-term impacts of a substance and to know what
effects it will have, particularly when it is combined with other

substances. There has been a tendency to give chemicals the benefit of the doubt and not classify them as hazardous unless substantial proof exists. As evidence of serious damage becomes clearer, many scientists are now saying that such risks should not be taken. In their report to the Canadian Environmental Advisory Council, Drs. Hall and Chant spoke out strongly on this issue:

> It is important to the understanding of the thesis of this report that most man-made chemicals cannot remain neutral in a living process. They are either a nutrient or a drug (poison). In the absence of precise evidence, we must assume that all man-made chemicals are poisons with power to modify, often irreversibly, the growth and life of all organisms.[17]

The Producers of Hazardous Wastes

RARE IS THE INDUSTRIAL PROCESS that does not generate some amount of hazardous wastes. Equally rare is the community that does not have within it a hazardous waste generator.

Ironically, it is frequently in the smallest and the supposedly non-industrial communities where generators of some of the most hazardous wastes are found. One of the factors in a company's decision to locate in a small town may be the access to open space. Such space makes waste disposal easier — plenty of empty places for open and covered pits and plenty of fields on which to spread wastes as though the wastes were manure. Tragically, easy access to space encourages the sloppiest of disposal practices.

The State of California's Office of Appropriate Technology has developed a priority listing of wastes whose disposal should receive the most concentrated attention.[18] This listing is based upon the wastes' toxicity, their persistence in the environment, their ability to bioaccumulate, and their degree of mobility in a landfill. These priority waste streams are pesticide wastes (insecticides, herbicides, and fungicides), polychlorinated biphenyls (PCBs), cyanide wastes, toxic metal wastes (for example, arsenic, barium, cadmium, chromium, lead, mercury, selenium, and silver), halogenated organics (chlorine, bromine, or fluorine combined with hydrocarbon compounds) and non-halogenated volatile organics (for example, hydrocarbon solvents, alcohols, aldehydes, and ketones).

Table 1 lists the industries that produce the six high priority waste streams. However, manufacturers in these industries are not the only ones who create these wastes. Users of these manufactured products are often sources of the same problem. For example, the local printing company that carelessly discards its used ink is throwing out toxic metals.

Table 1
Industries Generating the Six High Priority Hazardous Wastes

I: Pesticide Wastes

Manufacture of pesticides	Agriculture
Forestry	Structural pest control
Urban landscaping	

II: PCBs:
No longer produced or sold but large quantities are still present in insulating fluid for electrical equipment and are still a major disposal problem.

III: Cyanide Wastes:

Metal finishing (electroplating)	Electronics
Aerospace	Machinery industry
Mining	Metal-heat treating
Manufacturing	

IV: Toxic Metal Wastes:

Metal smelting	Pesticide Manufacture
Wood preservatives	Paint production
Electroplating	Battery manufacture
Chromate manufacture	Phosphoric acid production
Leather tanning	Textile production
Petroleum refining	Inorganic mercury compounds manufacture
Manufacture of alkyl lead compounds	Pharmaceuticals
Printing ink production	Photocopying equipment manufacture
Chlorine production in mercury cells	Copper, zinc and lead production
Electrical appliances	
Glass manufacture	

V: Halogenated Organics:

Industrial organic chemicals (e.g. solvents, refrigerants, aerosol propellants)	Electronics industry
	Aerospace industry
	Machinery industry
Plastics industry	

VI: Non-halogenated Volatile Organics:

Petroleum refining	Industrial inorganic chemicals industry
Plastics	
Industrial organic chemicals industry	Aerospace industry
	Machinery industry

Source: Compiled from the California Office of Appropriate Technology, *Alternatives to the Land Disposal of Hazardous Wastes.*

Current Hazardous Waste Generation
and Disposal in Ontario

NO ONE KNOWS HOW MUCH industrial waste is generated in Ontario each year. There are several reasons for this. The lackadaisical approach that society has always had towards wastes permeates industry. As a result, companies do not pay close attention to the quantities and kinds of wastes they produce. Some industries refuse to disclose their waste production because they fear that this will provide their competitors with useful information about their production processes. In addition, all industries and governments agree that some wastes are disposed of illegally and clandestinely. These wastes never appear on official inventories.

The Ontario Ministry of the Environment estimates that 50 million gallons of liquid industrial wastes are disposed of in Ontario each year.[19] But this figure substantially underestimates the amount of wastes actually produced. For one thing, solid wastes are not counted in this listing. In addition, the estimates of liquid wastes are incomplete because only those wastes hauled off the producer's property are recorded in the Ministry's figures. If a company disposes of its wastes without transporting them on public roads, there will be no government record. There is also some disposal of wastes that goes deliberately unreported.

The nature of this 50 million gallon quantity is controversial. Ministry of the Environment officials complain that when members of the public hear the words "liquid industrial wastes" they automatically assume that these wastes are hazardous.[20] Ontario's information collection system for wastes does not distinguish between hazardous and nonhazardous wastes. During an interview, the manager of the industrial section of the waste management branch of the Ministry of the Environment was asked to state which of the 23 categories of waste contain hazardous substances. Three of the categories, he said, are sure to be hazardous. On the other 20, he answered the question with terms such as "some", "very little", "most", and "a good part". In no instance did he say that a category could contain no hazardous substances.[21]

It's hardly surprising, then, that the reporting system in Ontario adds to the difficulty in assessing hazardous waste quantities. A little more light is shed on the situation by the federal government's 1982 estimates that Ontario's annual production of hazardous wastes was over six times higher than the 50 million gallons of liquid wastes stated by Ontario's Ministry of the Environment.

According to Environment Canada's *Canadian National Inventory of Hazardous and Toxic Wastes*, 320 million gallons of hazardous wastes are generated in Ontario each year.[22]

Of those liquid industrial wastes produced in the province, the disposal methods are reported for only the 50 million gallons identified by the Ministry of the Environment. Between April 1981 and March 1982, approximately 15 million gallons of liquid wastes were burnt at a temperature of almost 1500 degrees Celsius, in an incinerator in rural Lambton County near Sarnia.[23] Another 11 million gallons, approximately one-quarter of Ontario's liquid industrial wastes, were dumped into the eight landfill sites scattered across southern Ontario that are certified to receive such wastes. Other liquid industrial wastes were spread on farmland as fertilizer, dumped into private landfills, spread on roads as dust suppressants, and taken to municipal sewage treatment plants. Approximately 16 percent of the 50 million gallons was reused by industry in its production processes. In addition, approximately five and a half million gallons of liquid industrial wastes were taken to the United States. Some wastes were shipped the opposite way, but Ontario's Ministry of the Environment estimates that more wastes are sent to the United States than come into Canada.

Table 2 lists the Ontario facilities that have been licensed by the provincial government to receive industrial wastes.

Large quantities of wastes are legally disposed of by companies on their own property. Many industries, especially the larger ones,

Table 2
Certified Receivers of Ontario's Liquid Industrial Wastes, 1982

Facility	Location	Ownership
Incinerator	Lambton County	Tricil Ltd.
Incinerator	St. Catharines	Syntath
Landfill	Arnprior, Renfrew County	Municipally-owned
Landfill	Barrie	Municipally-owned
Landfill	Brantford	Municipally-owned
Landfill	Guelph	Municipally-owned
Landfill	Lambton County	Tricil Ltd.
Landfill	Mariposa, Victoria County	Municipally-owned
Landfill	Paris, Brant County	Municipally-owned
Landfill	Welland	Municipally-owned

dispose of their wastes by dumpⁱ   them into their own landfill
sites or lagoons, by burning them at an in-plant incinerator or by
spreading them on fields. Some companies have permits to dump
wastes into streams that flow through their property. In its 1982
studies, the Ontario Waste Management Corporation, a provincial
crown agency, estimated that one-fifth of the wastes generated by
Ontario corporations are disposed of on their own property.[24] The
Corporation estimated that another 25 per cent are discharged into
the sewage system.[25] These wastes tend to be ignored, but their
impacts upon the environment and upon people's health can be
just as dramatic as the effects of wastes that have been taken off
company property.

Solid industrial wastes can also be hazardous. However, the
Ministry of the Environment does not require special licensing for
the disposal of solid wastes. Most of these are dumped with regular
residential garbage into landfills throughout the province.

What happens to those components of Ontario's industrial
wastes that are considered by all parties to be hazardous? The
answer to this question is elusive. Many of those classified as
organics are burned in the Tricil incinerator near Sarnia, while a
smaller quantity are burned in St. Catharines. PCBs are generally

photo: Mark Trusz

*Lagoon facilities located adjacent to the Canagagigue Creek at the
Uniroyal plant in Elmira, Ontario.*

retained on the property of whatever company possesses them, or else sent to D&D Disposal at Smithville for storage, in both cases waiting for the provincial government to approve of a safe method of disposal or destruction. Approximately 40,000 gallons of PCBs are stored in above-ground tanks at the Smithville site just south of Hamilton.[26] Ontario Hydro has a facility 10 miles west of Toronto where 45,000 gallons of PCB wastes from its own electrical equipment are stored.[27] Other hazardous wastes are shipped to the United States. Still others are stored by companies waiting for the development of disposal facilities.

This does not account for all of Ontario's hazardous wastes. The Ministry of the Environment asserts that the Tricil landfill is the only landfill in Ontario that should be receiving hazardous liquid wastes. There is no doubt, however, that similar wastes are being disposed of at the seven other landfills that have been certified to receive what the government considers to be non-hazardous liquid industrial wastes. Solid hazardous wastes are disposed of at many landfills across the province.

Radioactive Wastes

OVER 80 MILLION TONS of radioactive wastes from uranium mining sprawl across 1800 acres near Elliot Lake, on the north shore of Lake Huron.[28] In some places, these hazardous wastes form a 30-foot high dull grey wall. The barren waste piles cover vast expanses that were formerly valleys, creekbeds, and lakes. Radioactive radium particles and radon gas blow off the piles. Along with highly acidic materials and ammonia, these radioactive substances wash into the surrounding streams. The nearby Serpent River is so contaminated by runoff from these waste piles that no fish have survived for 55 miles downstream.

At Ontario's nuclear power plants, 5,000 tonnes of highly radioactive wastes lie in temporary storage in water-filled pools.[29] Each Pickering-sized reactor produces an additional tonne of highly radioactive wastes every five days. As the wastes rapidly fill these pools, the government searches for a long-term solution. Storage in deep-wells in northern Ontario communities such as Atikokan and Massey has been suggested, but the local residents fear the unknown hazards that may be associated with such storage.

In March 1980 at Port Granby, Ontario, a collector reservoir at a dump overflowed, discharging 3,600 cubic yards of wastes contaminated with arsenic, radium, and uranium into Lake Ontario.[30] This dump contains an estimated 500,000 tons of radioactive wastes and contaminated equipment brought from Eldorado Nuclear Limited's uranium refinery at Port Hope, ten miles east of Port Granby. The edge of the dump is only 30 yards from Lake Ontario. Similar releases have occurred from this and other dumpsites for Eldorado Nuclear's radioactive wastes in the Port Hope area. Contaminated fill has been used on many construction sites in the town. A 1976 inspection found that one-third of the property in Port Hope had above-normal levels of radiation.[31] A separate school was closed when it was discovered that the children and teachers were being exposed to levels of radon gas up to twenty times higher than those considered safe by the federal government.[32] The radon gas came from loads of radioactive wastes used to fill in the ravine on which the school was built.

In Scarborough, a Toronto suburb, 4,000 tonnes of radioactive soil lie in the backyards of 32 families in a recently built subdivision.[33] The radioactive soil is the result of unsafe waste disposal practices 40 years ago by a company that used radium in the manufacture of aircraft instruments. Attempts to move the contaminated soil to the Canadian Forces Base Borden, near Barrie, to Bancroft, and to a Scarborough landfill have each been stopped. Citizens in the targeted communities immediately mounted vigorous campaigns to prevent their neighbourhoods from becoming radioactive dumping grounds. The radioactive soil still sits in the backyards of Scarborough families. One Scarborough resident, anxiously waiting for a suitable disposal site to be found, lamented, "Wherever you take it, it's someone's community."[34]

These are only a few examples of the potential and actual exposure of people and the environment to nuclear wastes, one of the most deadly of substances. Convinced of the potentially devastating health hazards posed by improper radioactive waste management, the Canadian Medical Association is considering a resolution criticizing the federal government for "allowing further development of uranium mining and reactor construction until a safe, proven disposal technology is developed for the wastes that have already been generated."[35]

The federal government and its agency, the Atomic Energy Control Board, are responsible for regulating and monitoring the handling of radioactive wastes. Their record in controlling these wastes and preventing problems has been no better than the records that we will examine of the provincial governments which are responsible for controlling the handling of all other wastes produced in Canada.

No acceptable methods for permanent disposal of radioactive wastes have been found. Nevertheless, large volumes of these wastes are produced daily. These nuclear wastes are a toxic burden whose hazards will last in some cases for a quarter million years. Although a different level of government is responsible for radioactive materials, the issues concerning their management are similar to those of other hazardous wastes.

The Health Effects

THE HEALTH EFFECTS of improper disposal of hazardous wastes are rarely immediately evident. The impacts may become obvious fairly quickly for the neighbours of a disposal site, but even in these cases controversy rages as to the cause and degree of their health problems.

In an article assessing water quality across Canada, Jane O'Hara pointed out the phantom nature of chemical pollutants:

> ... Odorless. Colorless. Tasteless, for the most part. Often they are present only in parts per billion. Toxic, in some cases. Carcinogens, in others. Mixing and mingling to form new chemical cocktails that are as yet unnamed.[36]

Not only are these cocktails unnamed — those who drink them or who inhale their fumes are usually unaware of their presence. And the scientists who test them are uncertain as to their contents and the immediate and long-term effects of these mixtures upon human health.

The full health effects of contact with chemical contaminants from an inadequate disposal site may not be felt for many years. Cancers usually do not arise until twenty years or more after contact with the cancer-causing agents. Some effects may not show up at all in this generation; instead, because of chemically-caused damage to parents' genes, the problem is passed on to future generations.

Exposure to chemical contaminants is a relatively new phenomenon since most of them are recent creations. Scientists are unable to predict what impacts this new phenomenon will have. They know little about which chemicals can cause cancer on their own, and even less about the hazards posed by combinations of chemicals. Despite this unknown impact upon human health, new chemicals are introduced into production processes daily.

In those areas near hazardous waste dumps where health surveys have been carried out, frightening patterns of health complaints are showing up. We shall look at two examples: the Love Canal area of Niagara Falls, New York and the Upper Ottawa Street area of Hamilton, Ontario.

During the summer of 1978, the thunderous, mist filled spectacle of Niagara Falls attracted its normal crowd of delighted tourists. Meanwhile, residents of nearby Love Canal were hardly amused by the sights that greeted them each day. Smelly black sludge oozed uncontrollably through basement walls. Backyards had unexplainable sink holes that turned into ponds filled with yellow, blue, and red semi-liquids. Fences collapsed when their foundations were eaten out. Gardens and shrubs withered and died. Their children played in the chemically-laden soil of the local schoolyard. Headaches, rashes, nausea, faintness and infections were becoming ever more common among the residents. That summer, the New York State Department of Health announced that it suspected the residents' health complaints were being caused by a toxic waste dump which had been abandoned 30 years earlier.

Dr. Beverley Paigen, a biologist and cancer researcher, then at Roswell Park Memorial Institute in Buffalo, gathered medical statistics on the residents around the Love Canal.[37] She assumed that contamination would be worst in the areas where old stream beds criss-crossed the Love Canal; these areas she called "wet areas". She compared people living in these areas with those who lived in other parts of the community. Her studies showed that people in the "wet areas" had unusually high rates of numerous ailments. The three most dramatic examples were:

- miscarriages occurred three times more frequently than in other parts of the community;
- birth defects occurred three times more frequently than in other areas; these birth defects included webbed toes, extra toe, unusually spaced teeth, deafness, mental retardation, kidney abnormalities, and heart defects;
- asthma occurred 3.8 times more often in the "wet areas" than in the other parts of the community.

Table 3 lists the other health problems that Dr. Paigen found were more frequent among residents she suspected were in contact with contamination from the old toxic waste dump. She concluded that these high incidences could only be explained by the effects of the Love Canal's wastes. "The Love Canal is as much a disaster area as any hurricane, earthquake, or flood," said Dr. Paigen.[38]

Preliminary chromosome tests on a random sample of people in the area revealed that just over 30 per cent of them had chromosome breakage of an extraordinary nature.[39] Such chromosomal damage is frequently linked to cancer and could lead to severe birth defects. Chromosomes are the genetic material passed on

Table 3
Health Hazards Detected at Love Canal

Miscarriages	Loss of coordination
Psychological depression	Headaches
Still births	Insomnia
Crib deaths	Hyperirritability
Birth defects	Cancer
Nervous breakdowns	Heart disease
Convulsions	Hearing loss
Epilepsy	Psychological depression

Urinary diseases (bladder infections, deformed urinary system)
Respiratory diseases (pneumonia, colds, asthma)
Skin diseases (rashes)
Immune response weakened (ear infections, colds)
Blood clotting impaired (nosebleeds, uterine, gastrointestinal and rectal bleeding)
Bone problems (demineralization resulting in weakening of bones)

Source: Compiled from Dr. Beverley Paigen, "Health Hazards at Love Canal," 1979.

from one generation to another; alteration of the chromosomes can result in the transmission of abnormalities to future generations.

The Love Canal tragedy goes beyond physical and biological problems. One thousand families were evacuated from the area, some permanently, others temporarily. It is impossible to measure the pain and family disruption that result from being forced from one's home. The stressful worrying about the long term impacts from exposure to chemical wastes continues even after moving away.

Michael Brown, author of *Laying Waste*, spent much time talking with people who lived in the Love Canal area. In the conclusion to his description of the Love Canal, he said,

> The psychological scars are bound to remain among both the adults and the children forever, along with the knowledge that, because they have already been exposed, they may never fully escape the Love Canal's insidious grasp.[40]

The tragedy of Love Canal is probably repeating itself in numerous other places. Hedy Gervais, a mother of two children, formerly lived across from the Upper Ottawa Street landfill in Hamilton, Ontario. Her experiences there led her to conclude: "It doesn't happen just in the United States. It can happen here — right in our own backyard."[41] The following is her description of conditions at that site before it was closed in 1980.

> The flames used to be about sixty feet in the air — it was just like a volcano erupting across the street. At the beginning I wasn't terribly concerned about those huge open fires. They seemed to be quite a way back and the smoke was blowing away from us. But then there became a point when we noticed a heavy chemical smell lingering in the air after the burnings. We became suspicious as to what they were actually burning over there.[42]

The people living in the townhouse complex across the street from the Upper Ottawa Street landfill investigated. What they thought was a harmless municipal dump turned out to be a 100-acre, 90-foot high mountain of garbage saturated with liquid industrial wastes. Two years after the dump had been closed to all new garbage, black tarry substances and dark coloured liquid continued to percolate through fissures in the clay cover that had been placed over the landfill. The air in the neighbourhood was still permeated by the smell of chemicals.

After persistent questioning by the residents, the Hamilton-Wentworth regional government admitted that sludges from a liquid waste solidification process at the site were dumped on the municipal garbage to speed up burning. Also, many of the liquid industrial wastes that had supposedly been brought for treatment were dumped directly onto the face of the landfill. Later it was alleged that among the wastes deposited at the Upper Ottawa Street dump were such highly toxic substances as PCBs and cyanide.[43]

Prompted by their suspicions that the health ailments among people living close to the dump were unusually high, the residents conducted an informal health survey with the assistance of two doctors from McMaster University. Although the survey could not conclusively show a connection between the dump and the health problems, the results did show that some health complaints were more frequent among those living near the dump than among people living a few miles away (See table 4). Hedy Gervais concluded: "We're being slowly and systematically poisoned, and our health problems will become more serious with the passing of time."[44]

For the Upper Ottawa Street citizens, the results were alarming. When they lobbied for a thorough health study, government officials announced that there was no cause for concern. Public pressure intensified as the revelations about what had been dumped at the site and the violations of government procedures developed from a trickle to a flood. A year later, in October 1980, the Ministry of Health announced that it would do an environmental and health survey. The persistence of the neighbourhood residents paid off, but the questions remain and the fears are far from over.

Table 4
Health Problems Near the Upper Ottawa Street Landfill

Problem	Near the Dump	West Mountain
Frequent sore throats	55	4
Frequent colds	32	9
Ear aches	47	3
Abnormal bleeding	20	4
Kidney problems	9	1
Skin rashes	29	13
Total population	127	134

Source: From a survey by Upper Ottawa Street Residents' Association carried out in November, 1979, as quoted by Betty Burcher, "No Love Canals Here," *Healthsharing.*

The types of health problems experienced by residents of the Love Canal and the Upper Ottawa Street areas are similar to those that are being or will be experienced by people living adjacent to other abandoned or improperly operated hazardous waste disposal sites. The seriousness of this problem is foreshadowed by the devastating consequences of past improper disposal. The "out of sight, out of mind" approach to waste disposal is sadly short-sighted. Tragically, our society is still caught up in the deceptive easiness of this approach, resulting in the continued negligent handling of vast quantities of hazardous wastes.

CHAPTER TWO
THE WASTE MANAGEMENT INDUSTRY

> I think we want to do it [dispose of wastes] legally. I think we want to
> do it in an environmentally acceptable manner. I think we want to do
> it as a service to industrial customers in a competent fashion. And I
> think we want to perform all of these things in a manner that is
> profitable to all our stockholders.[1]

WITH THESE WORDS a vice-president of Browning-Ferris Industries described the motivations behind the actions of the waste
management industry. Significantly, the bottom line was the making of profits.

The Structure of the Industry

THE WASTE MANAGEMENT BUSINESS is the preserve of a few.
Three companies, Browning-Ferris Industries, Inc. (BFI), Waste
Management Inc., and SCA Services Inc., dominate the industry in
North America.

Each of these companies started its business by winning municipal contracts to collect household garbage and by getting contracts to pick up and dispose of wastes generated by commercial
and industrial clients. As special handling of liquid industrial and
hazardous wastes became government requirements, companies
began offering new services to fill these needs. The backbone of
each company remains, however, the collection and disposal of
solid wastes. Their operations include pickup and transportation
services as well as disposal facilities.

These three companies expanded rapidly throughout North
America during the 1970's, primarily by buying out local companies. After acquiring a firm, the parent company would usually
award stock or the promise of a managerial position to the previous
president.

Founded in 1967 in Houston, Texas, with only one truck, BFI was
the largest waste disposal company in North America in 1980. It
operated at 150 sites in North America, Europe, and the Middle
East, thirteen of which are in Canada. The familiar dark blue gar-

bage bins with the large white initials "BFI" overflow with garbage in many communities. Over 3,000 trucks, 220,000 steel bins and 240 vacuum trucks are owned by BFI in addition to the 65 landfills it manages.[2] In 1981, BFI had a profit margin of 15.1 percent; the company's revenues exceeded expenditures by $48.5 million.[3] In an expansionary pattern typical of the company, BFI bought Sasso Disposal Ltd. of Windsor in 1972. Sasso Disposal had operated a waste pickup service and owned and operated the Ridge Landfill site in Harwich Township. This landfill received both municipal wastes and liquid industrial wastes. As part of the deal, the Sasso brothers were given positions in the new operation.

Waste Management Inc. of Oak Brook, Illinois, has undertaken a similar expansion. During the early 1970's, Disposal Services Limited and York Sanitation Company Limited operated competing landfills at Maple and Whitchurch-Stouffville, just north of Toronto. Within a period of two months, both companies were bought by Waste Management Inc. One of the previous owners of Disposal Services became a director of York Sanitation.[4] Currently the second largest waste disposal company in North America, Waste Management Inc. has 38 subsidiaries and associates including Waste Management of Canada Inc. The company had a profit margin of 20.4 percent in 1980, representing $54.9 million of revenue in excess of expenditures.[5]

SCA Services, Inc., the third largest waste management company in North America, does not operate disposal facilities in Ontario. Nevertheless, its New York State operations may have a profound impact upon Ontario's environment. The company's five-and-a-half mile long pipeline will pump treated liquid industrial wastes into the Niagara River. In the same fashion as BFI and Waste Management Inc., SCA Services has gone through rapid expansion. Formed in 1970 with headquarters in Boston, it acquired 130 small solid waste companies during its first three years of operation.[6]

BFI, Waste Management Inc., and SCA Services completely dominate the North American waste management industry. The 1981 sales dollars of these three companies, a total of $721 million, comprised 95 percent of the sales of the top 12 U.S. corporations involved in sanitary services.[7]

Two Canadian companies have been heavily involved in the disposal of liquid industrial wastes in Ontario: Tricil Ltd. and Laidlaw Transportation Ltd.

Tricil, jointly owned by Trimac Ltd. (a trucking company from Calgary) and Canadian Industries Ltd. of Montreal, disposes of liquid wastes at its incinerator and landfill near Sarnia. Tricil also operated an incinerator at Mississauga until it was closed down in 1978 because of violations of Ministry of the Environment standards. The firm is involved in municipal waste disposal as well. For example, it operates the Regional Municipality of Hamilton-Wentworth's disposal system which includes an incinerator, a landfill, and transfer stations. Tricil is the largest Canadian-owned waste management company with operations throughout Canada as well as in parts of the United States. Among these facilities is an incinerator for burning liquid industrial wastes near Mercier, Quebec. It is adjacent to the gravel pit from which leakage of chemical wastes has permanently contaminated a major supply of groundwater.

Until 1980, most liquid industrial waste facilities in the Hamilton area were owned by subsidiaries of Laidlaw Transportation Ltd. of Hamilton. Laidlaw owns highway transport, city cartage, waste management, passenger bus, and taxi services. About 25 percent of its revenue in 1981 was from its waste management operations. The company's profits were $13.8 million that year.[8] In 1982, Laidlaw announced that it was launching a major offensive in the U.S. to buy up waste management companies. It said, however, that it was going to steer clear of the liquid industrial waste business because of the "continuing controversy over the environmental effects of chemical waste disposal".[9]

Many small firms operate some form of waste disposal enterprise, including owner-operated trucking outfits. Nevertheless, it is the major companies that control most waste disposal in Ontario. The companies that have owned or attempted to develop liquid waste disposal facilities in Ontario between 1970 and 1982 are listed in Table 5.

The Business Climate

"HARD TO FIND DISCOURAGING word on outlook for Browning-Ferris" was the headline in a 1980 *Globe and Mail* business assessment.[10] This buoyant expectation for continued high profits and for growth, despite the recession that is hurting so many companies in North America, was based on two factors: the need for garbage to be collected "no matter what" and increased government regulation of liquid and hazardous wastes, which is making producing companies more dependent upon waste management companies.

Revenues from liquid and hazardous waste collection and disposal have increased dramatically reflecting acquisitions, new services and — more recently — increased regulatory attention. Browning-Ferris

Table 5: Private Involvement in Liquid Industrial Waste Facilities in Ontario, 1970 to 1982

I: Operating

Type	Location	Owner
Incinerator and Landfill	Lambton County	Tricil Ltd., owned by Trimac and Canadian Industries Limited
Incinerator	St. Catharines	Syntath
PCB Storage	Smithville	Chemical Waste Management, subsidiary of D&D Group

II: Closed

Type	Location	Owner	Year Closed
Deep-well	Lambton County	Tricil Ltd.	1976
Incinerator	Hamilton	Thermal Destruction subsidiary of Laidlaw Transportation Ltd.	1977
Incinerator	Mississauga	Tricil Ltd.	1978
Solidification plant	Hamilton	KD Enterprises, subsidiary of Laidlaw	1980
Landfill	Harwich Township	Browning-Ferris Industries	1981

III: Discarded Proposals for Facilities

Type	Location	Owner
Deep-well	Moore Township	Tricil Ltd.
Deep-well	North Gosfield Township	Sub-surface Pollution Control
Deep-well	Canborough	Cambrian Disposals Ltd.
Physical-chemical treatment plant and landfill	Nanticoke	Nanticoke Waste Management, subsidiary of D&D Group
Solidification plant	Harwich Township	Browning-Ferris Industries
Solidification plant	Thorold	Walker Brothers, subsidiary of S.C.M. Corp.

believes this regulatory function will play a major role in development of hazardous waste operations.[11]

Waste Management Inc. is also expecting an increasingly profitable future. It intends to expand its profits by getting into the business of cleaning up other companies' abandoned hazardous waste disposal sites.[12]

But not all is rosy. As of December 1980, lawsuits were lodged in the U.S. against BFI for a total of $30 to $40 million.[13] These lawsuits included government prosecutions for price fixing, bid rigging and violation of environmental regulations, and lawsuits by individual residents living near BFI sites for personal and property damages.

BFI is not alone in this predicament. Because of Love Canal, the federal and state governments in the U.S. brought a total of $700 million of suits against Hooker Chemicals. Compensatory and punitive damages totalling $16 billion were also being sought in 1982 by 1200 residents of the area.[14] Laidlaw's decision to stay away from the hazardous wastes business undoubtedly came from worries about the legal hassles that can result from problems at waste disposal sites.

In the U.S., the courts have gone beyond simply levying fines for pollution to actually compensating victims for damages from hazardous wastes. Companies have begun to search for ways to counteract this "black spot" that has the potential to rot away their profits. In the United States, companies are required to make contributions to a compensation fund called the Superfund, to cover costs for clean-ups and compensation. Legislation setting up this compensation system specifically states that company contributions do not take away the government's or private individuals' rights to sue the corporations involved. As a result, there will be a growing trend for companies to protect their profits by relying upon pollution liability insurance schemes.

The public's actions have become a major factor affecting the business climate of the waste management industry. These companies are being affected not only by public demands for compensation for damages incurred, but also by citizen group demands that facilities be set up properly before they are allowed to operate. As was shown in an instance in the Niagara area, this can prevent the quick profits to which waste management companies had grown accustomed.

A pipeline stretches five and a half miles from a chemical waste treatment plant in Porter, New York State to the Niagara River. It sat unused for almost two years until 1982. SCA Chemical Services

Inc. built the pipeline intending to discharge 100 million gallons annually of treated industrial wastes into the Niagara River. But citizens' groups objected to the plan. Fearing that the discharges would add to the pollution load of this already highly contaminated river, the citizens argued their case in lengthy public hearings. Located just two and one-half miles downstream from the pipe's outlet is the water intake for the Canadian town of Niagara-on-the-Lake.

In April 1982, after two months of private negotiations, the company, the New York State Department of Environmental Conservation, three environmental groups (Operation Clean of Niagara-on-the-Lake, Operation Clean of the U.S., and Pollution Probe of Toronto) and three municipalities came to an agreement on the pipeline. As a result of this agreement, a citizens' review board made up of environmentalists and municipal representatives was set up to supervise the testing of the pipe's contents and the effects of the discharges. The citizens' review board chooses the testing methods, the experts who carry out the tests, the laboratories where testing is done and the experts who interpret the results. No dumping, except for testing purposes, was to occur until the tests were completed; it was expected that this would take almost a year. Costs for the citizens' testing programme are fully paid by SCA.

The chairperson of Operation Clean (Niagara-on-the-Lake), Margherita Howe, said after the agreement, "SCA is becoming so pure, it is quite hysterical."[15] But she had no illusions about their motivations. They have been losing profits while tied up by citizens' groups for the past three years. "There is so much business in this area in hazardous waste disposal, between cleaning up old dump sites in the Niagara area and the current production of wastes by industry, that they can make millions if they operate properly," she said. "But we won't be taken in. We'll be watching them."[16]

The Industry's Safety Record

> The Ministry of the Environment think we're criminals. The public think we're dumpers. Companies think we're rip off artists.[17]

WITH THIS LAMENT, the owner of a small liquid waste hauling and disposal company near Barrie expressed the frustration of feeling that he is everyone's scapegoat.

The waste management companies claim that they are doing a fine job. The U.S. Chemical Manufacturers' Association, speaking about the problem of dealing with chemical wastes, said, "We who represent this industry have the knowledge and the technology to do the job. We have the commitment and the resolve."[18] Unfortunately, the record of these companies provides little basis for confidence.

During 1980, two reporters for Mississippi's *Clarion-Ledger* conducted a ten-month investigation of the largest of these firms, Browning-Ferris Industries.[19] The investigation revealed a long inventory of problems with BFI operations in the U.S. For example, it was discovered that on at least a few occasions when disposal trucks were washed out at a Louisiana site left-over toxic wastes were allowed to run into roadside ditches. At sites in Maryland, Louisiana, Texas, Kentucky, and Illinois, the firm has been accused of illegal and improper disposal methods. In Texas, oil containing large amounts of deadly cyanide and highly carcinogenic nitrobenzene was sprayed onto roads. At a BFI operation in North Carolina, a 17-year-old worker died when toxic fumes were released from chemical wastes. At another site, 30,000 gallons of wastes flowed from a BFI chemical waste storage tank into the water reservoir of Kernersville, North Carolina. The *Clarion-Ledger* reported that, when confronted by these problems and pressured to assume responsibility for corrective action, "Time after time, at site after site, BFI offers excuses, rather than action."[20]

Similar problems have occurred at Waste Management Inc. disposal sites. The company owns a landfill at Whitchurch-Stouffville, Ontario, from which contaminants, including PCBs, may be leaking into the water table, but company officials refuse to assume responsibility. In 1982, when finally forced by the Ministry of the Environment to take action to control future problems and to close down the dump, the company appealed the decision to the Environmental Appeal Board. It said that the minister acted because of "political elements". "He has been either seriously misinformed, perhaps misled, or simply mistaken in his findings."[21] The company has continued to resist taking action to protect its neighbours.

SCA's record is also laden with faulty operations and refusals to correct problems. The courts have closed down SCA facilities in parts of the U.S. and fined the company for disposing of chemicals illegally.

Nor are the two other large waste disposal companies operating in Ontario, Tricil and Laidlaw, free from controversy over their disposal practices.

After a court case in 1978, Tricil was fined $15,000 for failing to operate its Mississauga incinerator according to government standards. In response to residents' complaints, a Ministry of the Environment inspector had visited the site. Upon seeing heavy smoke coming from the stack, he ordered Tricil to stop emissions immediately by shutting down the operation. The shut-down could have been carried out within two minutes. But, as he walked away, the smoke continued to pollute the air. Carol Olchowsky, the lawyer who prosecuted Tricil on behalf of the government, said, "It did seem somewhat defiant, committing the offense in the man's face."[22]

In Quebec, Tricil's record has been equally spotty. In October 1982, Quebec's Environment Department charged Tricil with having illegally disposed of 3,500 gallons of liquid industrial wastes into a garbage dump northeast of Montreal.[23] In addition, serious questions have been raised about the adequacy of its incinerator near Mercier. Emission tests from the 150-foot high stack conducted in 1982 found that the quantities of particles being emitted were 13 times higher than the Quebec government's health standards.[24]

Subsidiaries of Laidlaw dominated the liquid waste disposal business in Hamilton during the 1970's. At their peak they operated a liquid waste incinerator in the Beach Strip area, a recycling operation on a harbour pier, and a landfill at Upper Ottawa Street, which, at one point, included a solidification process. A foreman reported that PCBs were burnt in the incinerator without government permission. Six lagoons were built to hold chemical wastes even though permits were again lacking. Without explanation, 150,000 gallons of liquid waste disappeared from one of the lagoons at the recycling unit; Ministry of the Environment officials suspected that the three 100-foot lengths of plastic hose found between the suddenly empty lagoon and the harbour were used to drain the lagoon. At the landfill site, 270,000 gallons of liquid wastes leaked out of the mixing and storage box at the solidification plant, through the bottom of a corroded tank known as "the magic box". After a lengthy court case, $13,000 in fines were levied against the company for falsifying waybill records. By the end of 1980, each of these facilities had been forced to close.

The U.S. Chemical Manufacturers Association assures the public that events such as the Love Canal will not occur again:

> As the story of Love Canal unfolded, a national symbol was born. However, the chance that a similar situation will occur is remote because of new legal requirements governing the placement, operation, and monitoring of waste disposal facilities.[25]

Significantly, the Chemical Manufacturers' Association does not place in industry its hope for a safer future; it says, instead, that it is government regulations that will provide the protection.

The members of the Ontario Liquid Waste Haulers' Association point out why companies cannot be relied upon to be self-monitoring. Even if a company wanted to provide an environmentally sound programme, they say, it would find itself pushed out of the field by competitors who are able to provide a cheaper service by not undertaking the more expensive measures that are necessary.[26] The search for profits outweighs the desire to provide environmentally safe services.

Chemical waste disposal companies have not developed public confidence in their ability to protect the environment from hazardous wastes. Discounting the possibility of corporate self-regulation, we examine in the next chapter the effectiveness of the Ontario government's controls program.

CHAPTER THREE
GOVERNMENT CONTROL
OF HAZARDOUS WASTES

IN 1977, THE ONTARIO Ministry of the Environment ordered a Cambridge area farmer, Howard Main, to discontinue his unlicensed liquid waste disposal business. No one knew how long he had been hauling industrial wastes from local companies and storing them on his farm. One of the demands made by Ministry officials was that he remove the wastes stored in a 10,000 gallon tank. Three years later, a *Globe and Mail* reporter discovered the tank was still full of chemical and metal wastes.[1]

Ministry officials were surprised when they were told the tank was still in use. They had assumed that the problem had been taken care of because of assurances from Main during telephone conversations.

The *Globe and Mail* reporter also discovered 70 metal drums full of chemical wastes in a field on the farm. The drums appeared to have been there for a considerable time as they were visibly deteriorating and allowing sludge to ooze out. However, two Ministry inspections had failed to discover them.

Instances such as these raise questions about Ontario's monitoring and enforcement system. The protection of the environment is made to rely on this government system because of industry's failure to deal carefully with the hazardous waste problem. Monitoring could enable the government to trace the production, transportation, and disposal of wastes. The development and enforcement of regulations and standards, a responsibility of the provincial government, could go a long way towards alleviating waste management problems. It is essential, therefore, to examine how the monitoring and enforcement system is working.

The Monitoring System
IN AN EFFORT TO ensure that hazardous liquid wastes are safely handled, Ontario's Ministry of the Environment has set up two programmes: 1) the waybill system and 2) the monitoring of waste

disposal and handling operations. The waybill system is intended to allow the province to keep track of where industry sends its wastes. The objective is to make sure that wastes end up in places where they will not cause environmental and health damage. Waste disposal and handling facilities are monitored to guarantee that government approved facilities are operated safely.

The Waybill System

Whenever liquid industrial waste is hauled off a generator's property for disposal, a waybill must be filled out. This form tells how much and what kinds of wastes were handled, who generated them, who carried the wastes and where the wastes were disposed of. Two of the five copies of each waybill are required to be sent to

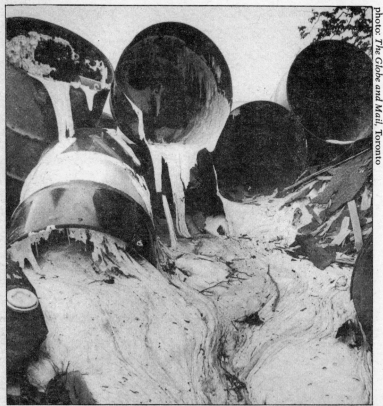

photo: *The Globe and Mail,* Toronto

Waste paint spilling from drums dumped on the property owned by Howard Mains near Cambridge, Ontario.

the Ministry: the one by the person who produced the waste and the other by the person who disposed of the waste. These copies are to be sent to the Ministry weekly.

Every two weeks, the Ministry checks to make sure that both copies of each waybill have been received. If it does not have both copies, the Ministry attempts to track down the missing wastes. In this way, the government hopes to be assured that all wastes are disposed of at suitable sites.

However, a 1980 investigation by Harwich Township revealed serious inadequacies with the province's waybill system. Using a search warrant, Township officials entered the offices of Browning-Ferris Industries in Windsor and at the Ridge disposal site; they seized copies of waybills in the company's files. An analysis of these waybills uncovered two startling facts:

- Seven months after they should have been sent to Toronto, Ministry copies of waybills for materials dumped at the Ridge Landfill were still in the carriers' or receiver's offices.[2]
- Twenty-five per cent of the waybills in the BFI records never showed up on the Ministry's listings.[3]

As a result, the Ministry had an incomplete picture of the amount and nature of wastes dumped in the Harwich landfill. When questioned at a public meeting as to how such a large discrepancy could have occurred, a Ministry official said, "Perhaps poor mail delivery is the cause of waybills not being received in Toronto."[4]

Even if these holes were plugged, problems would remain. The Ministry does not know that waybills are always used when they should be, and cannot be certain that the wastes are accurately described on those forms that are submitted.

Once a year, the Ministry sends each of its regional offices a complete printout of the wastes disposed of by each company in that region. The staff at the regional offices are expected to check whether the wastes shown correspond to the types and quantities of wastes that would be produced by each industry. It is understood that full knowledge about what is happening to wastes can only be achieved by knowing what is produced at the generators' level. While the intent is good, the reality is a different matter. A member of the Sarnia office of the Ministry described the situation:

> The problem is from the little guy who generates only one or two loads a year. If he doesn't show up in a year, I don't have any way of knowing. If there are a lot of them, I don't have the time to go around and check these guys.

> If you have small plants where there is maybe only a dozen work-
> ers and they may generate 10,000 gallons of wastes a year, if that guy
> gets a hold of somebody with a truck and that guy dumps that mate-
> rial in somebody's field, I'll tell you it is almost impossible to track it
> down.[5]

The waybill system relies upon the generator of wastes for its accurate functioning. It is unlikely that inaccuracies or deliberate deceptions will be detected and corrected in the system. The hauler of the wastes rarely notices inaccuracies. As a member of the Liquid Waste Haulers' Association said, "The hauler just knows what the company tells him."[6]

Most receivers of wastes do not check the contents of the materials, especially if the waste is going to be poured into a landfill. The receiver occasionally tests the wastes, but these tests are quite rudimentary and do not provide complete information. Finally, the government's monitoring system does not assure that the waybill form is used accurately.

"Everyone is playing a game of sham, because everyone has to play to stay alive," said one Ontario liquid waste disposer.[7] Industry's search for cheap disposal does not encourage faithful and accurate reporting of wastes. Stating that a waste falls into a hazardous category may result in having to spend much more money to dispose of it. For example, it is possible for a company to mix industrial waste with septic tank waste. Septic tank waste does not require a waybill and can be taken for cheap disposal at a sewage plant. It is also possible to fill out a waybill but check off a relatively harmless category, perhaps oily waters, and fail to note that part of the mixture is a much more hazardous substance, for example, PCBs.

In 1977, a Ministry of the Environment spokesperson said, "The story is that haulers dump illicit materials down sewers and into farmers' fields. We are not aware of any environmental catastrophes, but we have no doubt that it is going on."[8]

Six miles northwest of Barrie, hidden by bush, sit several tanks used in a recycling and chemical waste storage operation. In 1978, less than one year after their installation at the site, the rubber liners of two pits holding liquid industrial wastes started breaking down. An estimated 35,000 gallons of wastes leaked into the ground. Another 96,000 gallons were drained from the pits and loaded onto a tanker truck for disposal. The Ministry of the Environment thought that these wastes were taken to Sarnia for incineration. Four years after the dumping had occurred, however, a truck driver revealed that he had dumped these toxic chemicals into a landfill in Tiny Township, near Midland.[9] The wastes, said the driver, had been secretly dumped over three consecutive nights in accordance with instructions from Chemical and Petro Waste Disposal Ltd. of Barrie. When made aware of the wastes in the township dump, a Ministry official in the area said, "We did not question the report [of illegal dumping] as thoroughly as we might have."[10]

Even with compliance from all handlers of liquid industrial wastes, Ontario's present waybill system would give only a limited picture of what is happening to hazardous wastes. Solid wastes, wastes that are recycled, and wastes that are disposed of without being transported on a public road are not required to be reported. The volume of these three types of wastes is substantial. A 1982 federal government inventory estimated that wastes generated in Ontario are six times higher than those showing up in Ontario's waybill system.[11] Ontario has no system for reporting these quantities and their methods of disposal, but, if mishandled, each of these wastes can be hazardous to the environment and to people's health.

The objective of Ontario's waybill system — knowing what is happening to Ontario's liquid industrial wastes — is clearly not being fulfilled. Perhaps the most telling indication of the failure of this system came from the crown corporation that the Ministry of the Environment set up to develop a waste management system for Ontario. The Ontario Waste Management Corporation hired consultants to do a "Waste Quantities Study". When announcing this study, the communications director for the corporation said that they could not be sure of the reliability of the Ministry of the Environment's data.[12] His suspicions proved well founded; eight months later, the consultants reported hazardous waste volumes over six times higher than the Ministry's figures.[13]

Monitoring of Waste Disposal Sites

According to government officials, operators of waste disposal facilities have the primary responsibility for monitoring their own operations. A 1980 government report said:

> It is the function of the Ministry of the Environment to ensure that these [monitoring] programmes are adequate and carefully implemented, so that all aspects of the environment are protected.[14]

An example of the kind of monitoring undertaken at waste disposal facilities is the programme established at the Tricil incinerator and landfill near Sarnia.[15] Tricil takes monthly samples from nine wells on their property and three times a year from five other wells. Analysis of these samples is intended to provide warning of groundwater contamination. Samples collected by Tricil are split with the Ministry of the Environment, which uses its own laboratories for testing. The government also does some sampling itself. In addition, once or twice a year Ministry employees take samples from drinking water wells in the area.

On the incinerator stack is a mechanism that constantly monitors the particulate levels emitted into the air. These emissions are recorded on printout sheets which Ministry officials can ask to see. The Ministry of the Environment also has two monitoring stations — one up-wind and one down-wind of the incinerator. An annual study of vegetation and soil in the surrounding area is carried out by the Ministry to determine whether heavy metals, salts or other undesirable compounds are being added to the environment by the incinerator's ash emissions. Once a year, the Ministry's "super sniffer" or mobile air monitoring unit is brought in to test air quality.

The testing at Tricil has important shortcomings. On neither the stack nor on groundwater samples does the company or the government undertake a complete analysis for the presence of hazardous substances.

At the stack, the testing programme involves an analysis of total hydrocarbon content of the particulate emissions. Although there is a tremendous difference between the environmental hazards of various hydrocarbons, company officials note that "hydrocarbons are monitored but we can't tell specifically what the contents of those hydrocarbons are."[16]

The water quality testing at Tricil relies on testing for a limited number of chemicals. Unfortunately, testing the levels of only a select few chemical substances will not detect the presence of minute levels of many other particularly dangerous substances.

Testing like that conducted by the Ministry of the Environment and Tricil relies on analysis of individual chemicals in isolation from each other. Chemicals, however, do not act in isolation; they combine and react together to form unknown chemical substances, many of which may be hazardous. In addition, in recent years growing attention has been focussed on the synergistic effect of various chemicals, whereby the effects of one chemical combines with the effects of another to pose a greater environmental threat. The current testing programmes do not account for these possibilities.

Literally thousands of chemicals could be present in the leachate from a landfill or in the gases of an incinerator stack. To overcome the difficulties of testing for each individual material, the scientific community has developed simple biological tests, such as the Ames test, that can detect the presence of dangerous substances. Although these tests do not indicate the exact identity of the hazardous substance, they can indicate the need for additional and more thorough testing. This type of testing is not conducted at the Tricil facility.

The monitoring procedures followed at Tricil, despite their limitations, are more elaborate than at any other waste management facility in the province. Less adequate testing and monitoring is undertaken at the seven other landfill sites that are authorized to receive liquid industrial wastes. Concerns about the effectiveness of these monitoring systems are continually being raised.

During the summer of 1980, the Township of Harwich carried out a $145,000 investigation of BFI's Ridge Landfill in the farming area south of Chatham. For several months, three people carefully watched the operation. They used binoculars to see what was happening at the landfill, and followed trucks carrying wastes into the site. The surveillance even included airplane observation. The Reeve of the Township complained:

> As a result of the lack of Ministry of the Environment inspection, supervision, and control of the Ridge Landfill site, the township was obligated to conduct its own investigation. I feel this township should not have to do the job of the Ministry of the Environment.[17]

As a result of the township's investigations, numerous practices were found that did not follow Ministry guidelines.[18] The operator, BFI, failed to inspect many incoming loads at the gate to ensure these were handled properly and that government waybills were correctly filled out. Liquid wastes were dumped into open pits and left uncovered for months; Ministry regulations state wastes should be covered at the end of each working day. Frequently, waybills were not submitted by the carriers at the time they brought loads to the landfill.

According to workers at the dump, the Ministry would call BFI to tell them they were coming out to inspect.[19] The company had been known to tell the Ministry inspector, "It would not be convenient today. Why don't you come out next week?" The inspector would then make an appointment and the workers would spend the next few days cleaning up the site and covering wastes.

In addition to this, the township pointed out blatant violations of government regulations and of BFI's commitments as clearly stated on its application for a licence to operate a landfill.[20] The working area for wastes was to be at least 1,000 feet from the nearest public road; in fact liquid wastes were buried within 250 feet of the road. No wastes were to be disposed of within 3,000 feet of the nearest well, but one farmer's water source was only 500 feet from buried liquid wastes. Finally, the amount of liquids approved for burial at the site was regularly exceeded.

In another example of the failure of the province's monitoring programme, one and a half million gallons of liquid wastes were brought to the Walker Brothers quarry in Thorold during a four month period in 1979. The wastes, containing hazardous chromium, were trucked from the Ford Motor Company in metal drums and buried. A year later, a television reporter revealed what had happened. When the news was released, the Ministry director for that region said:

> I have no idea of what is in those drums. They could contain anything. Should a dig for the drums take place, the minstry would probably go as far as checking the contents of one representative drum.[21]

Incidents such as those at Harwich and Thorold lead the public to conclude that the Ministry's monitoring practices are inadequate. After all, neighbours say, if the inspectors are not at the site all the time, how can the government possibly know what is happening at the waste disposal site? Spot checks, especially if there is no element of surprise, are not a sufficient monitoring system.

When applications for approval of waste solidification plants in Harwich and Thorold were submitted in 1980, the government promised that a provincial environment officer would be assigned full-time to monitor each site. This promise was made in recognition of the public's lack of faith in the Ministry's monitoring programme. Unfortunately, this recognition has not led to the placement of full-time environment officials at the sites already handling industrial wastes in Ontario.

The Ministry's monitoring system relies heavily upon the company. The government says this is unavoidable. In 1980, Harry Parrott, then Minister of the Environment, said in the legislature:

> ... to have every/site on 24-hour inspection is impossible. It would take literally thousands of people and therefore would be impossible to do. I am not about to put 24-hour inspection on every waste site in Ontario that has a liquid waste certificate. It is that simple.[22]

Even when the government carries out monitoring programmes, the reports and test results are not automatically made public. After a lengthy effort, neighbours of the Upper Ottawa Street dump in Hamilton were unable to obtain site inspection reports. People who live next to potentially hazardous waste disposal sites do not understand why they have to fight to get such basic information from their government.

Sometimes, either deliberately or through incompetence, the Ministry misinforms the public. Farmers living next to the Ridge Landfill saw trucks going into the dumpsite with U.S. licence plates. They asked the Ministry of the Environment what wastes were being transported from outside of the country. The Minister insisted repeatedly that no wastes were being brought in from the U.S. Finally, the Ministry admitted that Eastman Kodak Ltd. of Rochester, New York, was shipping extremely hazardous chemical wastes from its photographic operations to Harwich. At the same time as the Minister was making his denials, the information had been in the Ministry's files.[23]

The results of comprehensive monitoring programmes that are made public do not necessarily end the uncertainties. Their interpretation is frequently a source of controversy.

According to the Ministry of the Environment, the landfill site at Whitchurch-Stouffville has been tested more than any other site in Ontario.[24] But the large number of water tests — 25,000 — has not resolved the public's concerns about the quality of drinking water in their wells. Tests in the mid-1970s showed what the Ministry of the Environment described as a "chemical imbalance"; the local residents called it "pollution".[25] "It has become a word game," said Fran Sainsbury, a real estate agent and farm dweller in the Whitchurch-Stouffville area.[26] Describing the Ministry's interpretation of test results, she said:

> Everytime there is a high spike [a rise in the figures], they [the Ministry] call it a perturbation or an anomaly. But when it drops back, they say "Now we have another downward trend."[27]

The people of Whitchurch-Stouffville accuse the Ministry of deliberately downplaying the results through its interpretations.

People in the Hamilton area have also raised questions about the interpretation of monitoring results. In February 1982, preliminary results of air monitoring tests at the closed Upper Ottawa Street dump were released. Dr. Joseph Cummins, a geneticist at the University of Western Ontario, described the report: "My conclusion is that the report has gone so far not to be alarming that it is rather misleading."[28]

Mercury was found in the well water on some farms around the Ridge Landfill. Originally, Ministry officials told the people drinking from those wells that the only acceptable level of mercury in water was none at all, but, when mercury was found, the Ministry said it was within acceptable guidelines. Lillian Tomen, who lived next to the landfill, asked, "Are the acceptable levels going to increase as the metals in the water increase?"[29]

The Hamilton Experience

During the late 1970's, controversy raged in Hamilton over the local handling and disposal of liquid industrial wastes. The revelations that emerged provide a telling summary of the failure of the province's monitoring programme. In November 1978, the top Ministry of the Environment official in the Hamilton region assured everyone that there were no problems with toxic wastes in the Hamilton area:

> They're [Interflow] carrying out a pretty straight-forward operation.
> All of their operations are on the up and up as far as I can determine.[30]

Over the next two years, each of the hazardous waste management facilities in the area was forced to close because of unsatisfactory performances.

During this two year period, the Ministry made statements based upon their monitoring that contrasted sharply with revelations coming out of the community:

- In February 1978, the Ministry's regional official "praised the results of an experimental [solidification] process conducted at the dump."[31] It was later discovered that 270,000 gallons of toxic wastes, the equivalent of 12 backyard swimming pools full, had leaked out of the box used to hold and mix materials for solidification.

- In November 1978, the same official said that he knew "what was going into the site on an annual basis."[32] Nevertheless, because of pressure from the opposition parties in the legislature, the government did a special audit of three months of waybills at the Interflow transfer station, requiring 44 staff days. They were unable to account for the final destination of 540,000 gallons of chemical wastes received during that period by the company. This was one-third of the wastes received by Interflow during that three-month period.

- Only wastes produced in Hamilton-Wentworth were to be taken to the solidification process at the Upper Ottawa Street Landfill. The three month audit showed that less than half of the wastes taken to the solidification site were from within the region. Environment Ministry officials admitted that two years earlier they had known wastes were being brought in from outside of the region,[33] but they had not stopped the practice and had not informed the community of this violation.

- Thirty-five waste haulers had keys to the dump;[34] under the *Environmental Protection Act* it is illegal for haulers to have keys to a site.
- Environment Minister Parrott told nearby residents that the materials at the site would not cause health problems. "Most of the liquid waste that went into the landfill site consisted of water used to wash industrial tanks that held substances like oil, caustics and rust preventative materials," he said.[35] One worker at the operation said, however, that he knew one hundred 45-gallon drums of PCBs had been dumped into the site and that large amounts of cyanide and wastes from the production of pesticides were regularly dumped there.[36]

The Ministry had done "spot checks on Interflow, KD [KD Enterprises, operators of the solidification plant] and the landfill site in 1976 and 1977," according to Parrott. "In the first eight months of 1978, staff conducted limited investigations and indeed even tailed company trucks."[37] But the Ministry consistently said there were no problems during this period. All this information about dumping practices at the site was first discovered by people outside of the Ministry. These outside pressures forced corrective action.

In a July 1977 report on the Upper Ottawa Street landfill, a laboratory employee of the regional government said he was "horrified by the nature and amount of the materials [dumped]."[38] Despite this statement and evidence of contamination shown in the provincial government's own testing programmes, assurances were given that there were no health problems. When metal contaminants were discovered in a nearby creek, the medical officer of health for the region said, "It turns the stream black and will kill some fish, but it doesn't constitute a health hazard."[39] In March 1980, the Minister of Health said, "The residents of the subdivision bordering Upper Ottawa Street opposite the landfill site are separated from the deposited wastes by several hundred feet and they would have no direct physical contact with the deposited material."[40] Six months later, because of public pressure and the proof of unsafe practices at the site, he announced an extensive health study for the area.

The people living around the dump wondered what was going on. The province's monitoring system consistently assured them that there were no problems, but after revelations from other sources, the Ministry always ended up reversing its earlier position, often within a few weeks or even days. Hedy Gervais, one of the mothers who had worked with the citizens' group in the area, was distressed by the failure of the government's monitoring system:

> We had trouble understanding why they [the Ministry of the Environment] weren't more strict. That's the question: Why?[41]

The Enforcement Programme

MONITORING WITHOUT RIGOROUS ENFORCEMENT is meaningless. If monitoring indicates problems with a particular waste management operation, three types of action are available to the Ministry. The first option is to negotiate improvements and issue control orders. The second is to undertake legal prosecution. The third is to revoke the company's certificate of approval to operate or else to issue a stop order.

The Ministry of the Environment views negotiation as the first step in the enforcement programme. At a public inquiry into waste management operations in Maple and Stouffville, an employee of the Ministry said:

> It is the function of this Ministry not to close down sites but to try and obtain co-operation in the proper operation of sites and as a result it is Ministry policy to use the administrative structures provided in the Act [the Environmental Protection Act] before resorting to prosecution in most cases.[42]

Regional and district officers of the Ministry of the Environment attempt to remove or alleviate problems that arise by having discussions with the individual companies involved.

If the Ministry's officials are not satisfied with the co-operation they are receiving from the company, the Ministry may issue a control order. Control orders state conditions with which the company must comply. If the company fails to comply, it is breaking the law and can be taken to court or may have its operating certificate removed.

Sometimes local residents provide the pressure that leads to control orders being issued. This was the case at the Tricil disposal facility near Sarnia in 1978 where emissions from the 225-foot high stack of the incinerator were causing considerable smoke and smells. Neighbouring farmers were complaining not only about these emissions, but also about problems from the open pits into which liquid chemical wastes were poured. After heavy spring rains one year, a dyke on the property broke, releasing chemical wastes which destroyed vegetation and killed mud turtles after flowing into a municipal ditch. In another incident, materials from the landfill ran into a neighbour's field killing his corn crop. In this case Tricil was obliged to remove the contaminated topsoil.[43] Following these incidents, local residents and the township government increased their pressure on the Ministry to take action.

Lengthy talks were held between the Ministry and Tricil. Finally, a control order was issued.[44] It required improved venting on tanks to control smells and the installation of on-line monitoring devices in the incinerator stack, and also set minimum temperatures for burning wastes. The order required the closing down of the incinerator when weather conditions were such that the plume from the stack would return to the ground. In addition, the order limited the size of the open pits into which wastes were poured.

Negotiations leading to control orders occur privately between the company involved and the Ministry of the Environment. No opportunity is given for input from residents or from municipal politicians. Frequently, the local people are not even aware that a control order has been issued or of the precise conditions of the order.

The fact that the public, including local councillors, are not privy to these negotiations fosters their suspicion about the basis for the government's decisions. Is the deciding factor the welfare of the environment and the people, or the ability of the company to keep operating?

Compliance with Ministry wishes cannot always be achieved through negotiations and control orders. Sometimes it is necessary for the government to take a company to court in order to protect the environment. Carol Olchowsky, a Ministry lawyer, found that prosecution is sometimes the only way to change a company's behaviour:

> We had one operator of a landfill site that was chronically violating the order issued against him and we took him to court. The first time he was fined a thousand dollars; he improved somewhat but slipped back. The next time, fifteen hundred; a little bit of improvement but he slipped back. Next time, ten and half thousand dollars! Perfection since! If the Ministry says, "Jump," he says, "How high?"
>
> There's a few people that need that heavy fine. With many people, laying charges is enough.[45]

Fourteen cases were prosecuted between January 1980 and May 1981. Approximately one-half of these prosecutions were for using a facility for waste disposal that did not have proper approval from the Ministry. The other half were for violations of the waybill system. In each case, the accused pleaded guilty or was convicted. The following are some examples of Ontario prosecutions for violations of waste disposal regulations.

- A & A Liquid Waste Removal Co.: convicted of burying tankers in a gravel pit near Maple without Ministry approval. The tankers were used to store and treat liquid industrial wastes. Fine: $6,000.
- Chemical Leaman Tank Lines Inc.: convicted of transporting liquid industrial wastes in Hamilton without a permit. Fine: $3,200.
- Brown's Septic Service: convicted of mixing industrial wastes from American Can in Niagara Falls with sludge and disposing of it as if it were domestic sewage sludge. Fine: $500.
- Scientific Sanitation: used an unapproved truck for transporting liquid industrial wastes and dumped waste in a Windsor scrapyard. Fine: $750.
- Western Metals Corp. Ltd.: this scrap metal dealer in Thunder Bay drained transformer fluid containing PCBs into a hole on his property. Fine: $7,000 plus cleanup costs. Superintendent fined $2,500.
- Tricil: convicted of allowing excessive air emissions from its incinerator at Mississauga. Fine: $15,000.
- Interflow Systems Ltd.: convicted on 13 charges of falsifying waybills. The origins of wastes sent to the Upper Ottawa Street dump in Hamilton were falsely stated. Fine: $13,000.
- Nacan Products Ltd.: convicted for failing to follow the provisions of the waybill system. Between 700 and 1000 drums of liquid industrial wastes were sent from Toronto on an unlicensed truck to an unlicensed landfill in Boucherville, near Montreal. Fine: $5,000.

Although the Ministry has prosecuted some offenders, the public's experiences lead them to believe that the Ministry is reluctant to prosecute. In the case of the chaotic waste handling operations in Hamilton in the late 1970's, it was the persistent raising of concerns by the neighbours in the area and by the leader of the Liberal Party in the legislature that brought an investigation and the eventual laying of 138 charges against the companies involved.

After his examination of waste management practices in the Maple and Whitchurch-Stouffville areas in the 1970's, Judge Hughes expressed sympathy for the frustrated feelings he had witnessed there:

There is no doubt in my mind that a great deal of justifiable public resentment was occasioned by the spectacle of dump trucks rattling past the building where a hearing was convened to entertain an application for authority to do what their owners were doing without any authority whatsoever, and by open violation of orders made by a ministry of the government on the grounds that either an appeal was pending or the officers of the ministry were trying to coax a recalcitrant operator into a mood of compliance with what had been ordered.[46]

The infrequency of prosecutions combined with the seemingly small fines for those who are prosecuted have made many citizens dubious as to the effectiveness of this part of the government's enforcement system. Stop orders and revocations of certificates are the most stringent actions that can be taken by the Ministry. These measures can be used if the danger to health and the environment is so severe that further risks cannot be permitted. As of 1982, neither instrument had been used to control hazardous waste facilities.

Limitations are built into these methods, which substantially reduce their potential effectiveness and the likelihood that the government will use them.

If the Ministry announced the revocation of a certificate, the company would have the right to appeal the decision to the Environmental Appeal Board. Months would likely pass before this hearing was carried out and a decision was made. In the meantime, the company would be allowed to continue releasing its questionable wastes.

A stop order would bring an immediate end to the operation of a facility. The government is hesitant to use a stop order, however, since the company may challenge the order in court. If the court decided that the situation was not an emergency as claimed by the government, the company would be given an award for damages. This potentially costly award would include recompense for profits lost during the time that the company was closed down.

The Controls

EVEN IF ONTARIO HAD a thorough monitoring system and strictly enforced the present laws, regulations, and standards, future hazardous wastes problems would not be avoided. As it stands now, many actions are permitted that are potentially destructive to the environment.

Chemicals have escaped even from legally operated waste disposal sites. The wastes buried in plastic-lined pits in 1969 by Uniroyal at Elmira, which threaten to contaminate the Grand River system, were buried under government supervision. Uniroyal currently sends many of its wastes to Elmira's municipal sewage plant for treatment. Tests in the creek below the point where treated wastes are released from this sewage plant have found increased chemical contamination sufficient to lead a Ministry spokesperson "to be concerned".[47] But this treatment was carried out with the Ontario government's approval and supervision. The river's contamination reflects the inadequacy of control measures designed by the provincial government.

The current laws and guidelines have several major flaws. One is acceptance of the idea of limitless waste production. Government regulations have focused on requirements for the handling of wastes, including restrictions on the use of certain disposal techniques. Experts estimate that between 40 and 80 percent of industries' hazardous wastes can be avoided through waste reduction and recycling.[48] The government has not, however, pushed companies to recycle and reduce their wastes. Joe Castrilli of the Canadian Environmental Law Association reported:

> Federal and Ontario laws are especially lacking in the areas of waste reduction, reuse, reclamation, recovery, and related management options. Indeed, these matters are conspicuous by their absence from Ontario's seven point program on industrial waste. This is not surprising since the program is centred almost exclusively on disposal.[49]

The government's failure to use strong legislation and incentives to reduce the wastes produced has meant that the most effective means of avoiding hazardous wastes problems is not being used to its potential.

In some instances, the government has passed legislation to protect the environment, but has not put it into force. In December 1979, the province passed the spills bill, which is designed to ensure the clean-up of hazardous wastes spills and provide partial compensation to those harmed by spills. As of October 1982, almost three years later, this act had not been proclaimed and the regulations needed to enforce it had not been passed. Therefore, though sitting on the books, the legislation could not be used.

When inadequacies in legislation have been pointed out, the Ministry of the Environment has sometimes promised revisions. But it has been slow at making such changes. In October 1978, a committee of the provincial legislature recommended changes in the waybill system. Four years later, no changes had been made despite the admission by the Director of the Waste Management Branch that "the waybill is limited and needs improvement."[50] In another example, the province promised in October 1978 to set up a perpetual care fund for the clean-up of existing and inactive or abandoned sites. Once again after four years no action had been taken.

Government standards for allowable emissions pose another serious problem. These standards have two major flaws. They are often criticized for not being strict enough, and they do not take into account factors such as cumulative and combined effects. The International Joint Commission in its 1982 report on Great Lakes water quality described these standards and measuring systems as "the Achilles heel" of government control strategies.[51] The other major problem with these standards is that they are usually suggested guidelines rather than regulations. As a result, they have no force in law unless the government writes them into a company's licence for a particular facility as a condition of operation. Generally, this is not done unless the operation becomes such a threat to the environment that a control order is issued. The use of standards or guidelines rather than legally enforceable regulations means that the public is unable to take a company to court for excessive emissions.

In an October 1982 speech, federal environment minister John Roberts described the inadequacy of the present government approach. He said that the existing system of legislation, regulations and standards "always means playing catch-up with pollution and polluters", rather than being "advocates" for a clean environment.[52]

Ontario is not the only government whose approach is not adequate for protecting the environment. In August 1982, when criticised by environmental groups for failure to fulfil its promises around hazardous waste disposal, Ontario's environment minister Keith Norton defended himself by saying that Ontario was further ahead than the other provinces in dealing with the problem of hazardous wastes. Unfortunately, Norton's statement was accurate. But the International Joint Commission's 1981 report on water quality in the Great Lakes put this statement into perspective by concluding:

> Legislation exists to control the manufacture and use of toxic substances in the Great Lakes Basin. However, the development and implementation of programs under the laws have been slow.[53]

The Government's Perspective

WHEN SURPRISED, CONFUSED, AND CONCERNED about possibly hazardous wastes in their communities, people turn for answers to their natural ally — their government. They assume that this body has the expertise to assess the situation and find solutions. It is also assumed that, since it is the public who elects the government, it will put citizens' health and the well-being of the environment above all other concerns.

Governments try to reassure the public that they know what is going on with hazardous wastes and that everything is under control. But those who are confronted by the problems of toxic wastes in their neighbourhoods know that this is not the case. When government officials downplay an obviously serious situation, their authority is invalidated in the eyes of those who are directly affected by these problems. In an editorial, the *Globe and Mail* concluded:

> The questions are inescapable: What do we have an Environment Ministry for? What do we have an Environmental Protection Act for? Why does the government of Ontario even bother paying lip-service to the value of preserving a moderately healthy world? In practice, they belie their principles at almost every move. Perhaps they are fooling themselves, but they are fooling no one else, and — far, far worse — they are jeopardizing the safety and the lives of us all.[54]

The recognition that all is not well combined with indifferent and unco-operative responses from the government has led many citizens to conclude that government is more interested in protecting industry than in protecting the public.

From her kitchen window, Sherry Morrison can see the plume of emissions coming day and night from the stack of the Tricil incinerator in Lambton County. She used to call local Ministry of the Environment officials, asking them to check the emissions on days that they were particularly smelly or unusually coloured. At first she was simply dismissed by the Ministry and felt like "a little old dumb lady. If they could have shut me up on the phone, I am sure that would have been it."[55]

When the Ministry realized that Sherry Morrison and her neighbours would be persistent, it started to pay attention. The Ministry did finally issue a control order on the Tricil operation, but its reputation had already been irreparably damaged in the eyes of the community. They believed that the Ministry's prior commitment was to the company. "The Ministry always seems to be in the role of protecting the industry from our questions," Morrison said, "rather than protecting us from the possible hazards coming from industry."[56]

The people of Harwich had similar experiences with the government. The Ridge Landfill received liquid industrial wastes for 12 years. Those living around this landfill observed worrisome occurrences: the galvanizing was being eaten off drainage pipes, unusually coloured liquids flowed through ditches, dead ducks were found in these ditches, and fish were seen jumping out of the stream and dying on shore. Whenever residents called the Ministry of the Environment to send inspectors, they had to wait.

When the local people pushed the Ministry for answers to their concerns, they were repeatedly rebuffed. When shown the coloured water in ditches adjacent to the landfill, the Ministry inspector would say "prove that it comes from there." When traces of mercury and arsenic showed up in well water, the Ministry would say that the chemicals were not necessarily linked with the landfill. The citizens had to push the Ministry to release results of tests that had been done at the site. Diane Jacobs was one of those people who persistently struggled for responses. Her experiences led her to conclude, "Government believes industry. The people have to prove what they say. Business is number one."[57]

The fact that governments appear to be on the side of industry is partially explained by their shared perspective. Virtually all governments have accepted the ideas that growth is essential, that increasing waste production is an inevitable by-product of growth, and that interference with corporate decision-making would destroy the economy. Accepting the notion that decision-making should be based upon profit levels, governments try to minimize their interference in that aspect of corporate affairs. Companies argue that stricter controls would force them out of business, a threat that puts considerable pressure on governments not to act. Uniroyal executives subtly threatened to move their chemical plant out of Elmira if environmental regulation became too severe: "We've put a lot of money into staying on top of this thing [waste disposal] and a lot of effort, but there's a limit, obviously."[58]

Some people suspect that the commonality of interest between industry and government goes beyond a common perspective. One person searching for an understanding of why government has become a barrier to an effective waste management system said, "After all, who feeds that government? Industry!"[59]

Government officials often react defensively to any suggestion of problems with waste disposal. Rather than approaching the question as a matter to be openly investigated, they seem to approach it with the objective of showing that there is no problem. After their debate with the government over water testing, the people of Whitchurch-Stouffville concluded, "They [the Ministry people] are political. They are looking not to find things, in order to protect their political backsides."[60] Admitting that problems exist becomes an admission that they have failed in the past.

The Whitchurch-Stouffville Water Quality Debate

IN 1981 AND 1982, the longstanding debate over Waste Management Inc.'s landfill in Whitchurch-Stouffville reached a climax. This stage of the debate provided a detailed illustration of how the government acts when it is caught in a controversial situation.

During the period from 1962 to 1969, thousands of tons of toxic liquid industrial wastes were poured into a landfill located on a porous moraine just north of Whitchurch-Stouffville. One particular hole on the site was called a "garbageman's delight" because "you could pour stuff in one day and when you came back the next it was empty."[61] After 1969, the landfill was only permitted to receive non-liquid wastes.

For many years, local residents questioned the Ministry of the Environment about the impacts of the wastes in the landfill on groundwater located only 100 feet below the dump. This water was tapped by nearby residents' wells and supplied the town of Whitchurch-Stouffville. In the spring of 1981, a group of Whitchurch-Stouffville mothers noticed an unexpectedly high number of miscarriages. When they conducted health surveys of their neighbourhood, they found high incidences of many disorders. Some of them suspected that these health problems could be caused by their water supply being contaminated by the landfill. Ministry of the Environment officials, however, assured them that there were no such links. On the basis of "the most comprehensive testing of any water supply in the history of this province, using some of the most sophisticated methods available to us," Minister of the Environment Keith Norton concluded that there was "outstanding water quality in the community" of Whitchurch-Stouffville.[62] But the local citizens remained unconvinced.

Dissatisfied with their dependence on the Ministry of the Environment for testing and interpretations, Whitchurch-Stouffville residents sought outside experts. Elaine Fritz, of the local citizens' group, explained: "We started doing our own tests because we were tired of arguing with them [the Ministry of the Environment] over what tests should be done."[63] Throughout the following year, the Concerned Citizens of Whitchurch-Stouffville spent almost $9,000 on testing; they raised this money through individual donations, bake sales, and benefits. The laboratories that they contacted — Advanced Environmental Systems Inc. of New York State (a lab that did extensive testing at the Love Canal), Dr. Joseph Cummin's lab at the University of Western Ontario, London, and Chemical and Geological Laboratories of Calgary — produced results that seriously questioned the Ministry of the Environment's conclusions about Whitchurch-Stouffville's water quality.

A vigorous debate between the Ministry and local citizens ensued. Fran Sainsbury, one of the residents involved in that debate, said, "The Ministry of the Environment tried to invalidate us, and to harass and intimidate us and the scientists who did our testing."[64]

The Ministry's way of challenging the work of the scientists involved went beyond scientifically questioning results and techniques to the point of making embarrassing and inaccurate statements. In the provincial legislature, Keith Norton said that the Calgary lab was about to fire the employee who had conducted the testing for the citizens of Whitchurch-Stouffville.[65] This was denied by the manager of the Calgary lab. In another instance, an official at the Ministry's lab sent a letter to the geneticist from the University of Western Ontario who had conducted tests for the citizens. This letter said:

> I find it astonishing that you saw fit to publicly criticize the study design, especially since all the scientists involved have taken such pains to render it as rigorous and scientifically sound as possible. On behalf of the Ministry scientists involved in the study, I want to register their anger and dismay that you resorted to such steps in advance of the study's completion.[66]

A copy of this letter was sent to the President of the University in an obvious attempt to embarrass the faculty member.

In addition to challenging the scientists involved, the government attacked the media and the local citizens. The *Toronto Star* had reported extensively on the Whitchurch-Stouffville water quality debate. In December 1981, Norton condemned the *Star*'s coverage suggesting that the reporter covering the story be transferred to Harlequin Books "where he could better apply his skill at fiction."[67]

On February 4, 1982, Fran Sainsbury was asked to come to the downtown Toronto offices of the Ministry of the Environment. She was asked to dissociate herself and the Concerned Citizens of Whitchurch-Stouffville from the test results of the Calgary lab. A sheet of paper was presented to her, unsigned and with no letterhead, listing a series of retractions that Ministry officials wanted her to issue in a press statement. She refused.

A month later, the Environment Minister held a 90-minute press

You Never Miss Your Water
Till the Well Ain't Fit To Drink

by Dennis O'Toole

Chorus: Up in Whitchurch-Stouffville
      There's a whitewash goin' down:
      They call it "sanitary landfill"
      While they're poisoning the ground.

It's a classic case of cover-up
An issue clouded in smoke
Those that finally woke and spoke up
Are getting passed off as a joke.

Yes, the province turns a deaf ear
To the cries of concerned folks
Not as worried 'bout their welfare
As catering to the corporate hoax.

Don't you tell me 'bout my water, son,
I wouldn't want to hear;
How could anything be unsafe
That looks so pure and clear?

I used to think, "Lord it can't happen here"
Now you've laid it in my lap;
What's it come to when you've got to fear
The very water from your tap?

repeat chorus: Up in Whitchurch . . .

"Nonsense!" cried the jolly banker
It's a foolish tale they tell;
Sure we welcomed every tanker
But don't you worry 'bout your well.

"Is it true?" cried Mr. Restaurant
You just can't tell by the taste,
I try to give the folks what they want
I'd hate to serve toxic waste.

Why are these folks up in arms?
Who's raising all the fuss?
Is there any cause for alarm?
Is it really up to us?

"You're damn right," cried the worried mother
Who'd just lost her unborn son;
If we can't take the time to bother
Has the end really begun?
repeat chorus: Up in Whitchurch . . .
Don't you tell me 'bout my water, son,
I wouldn't want to hear;
How could anything be unsafe
That looks so pure and clear!

---

briefing at which he released a three-volume critique of the citizens' testing programme. The critique was accompanied by a threat. "Those who choose to make loose-lipped allegations about the staff of this ministry," said Norton, "could find themselves being held accountable.... There are laws relating to slander."[68] Fran Sutton responded to this statement on behalf of the Concerned Citizens of Whitchurch-Stouffville: "His threat is very intimidating, but it is not going to stop us going on. We are going to continue to fight."[69]

The people's determination was based on their lack of confidence in the Ministry's answers. For example, the explanations given for the presence of hazardous substances found in the water were disconcerting for those who drank it. At one point, the Ministry of the Environment reported that tests had found PCBs in one borehole. Four months later the Ministry said that there were no PCBs in the samples. "The preliminary low PCB results were due to contaminated laboratory glassware and did not reflect actual subsurface PCB levels," the government explained.[70] This explanation did not increase local confidence. "They can't have it both ways," said Fran Sainsbury. "Now we say there is either PCBs in the well at the site or there is poor quality control in the Ministry's labs."[71]

In other cases, tests found contaminants in the water supply; even though similar substances were known to be in the landfill, the government insisted that the landfill was not the source of the contamination. Fran Sutton said, "They seem to be ignoring the most obvious possibility — the landfill — and centring on less obvious possibilities."[72] Another resident said, "If you smell smoke and the house beside you is in raging flames, do you get in your car and go driving down the road looking for the fire?"[73]

The citizens questioned not only the quality and the interpretation of some of the Ministry's test results, but they also challenged the whole basis of the monitoring programme. Their dissatisfactions included:

- the carrying out of routine water analyses and tests for individual chemicals, but not overall tests for mutagenicity and carcinogenicity,
- the failure to take into account possible synergistic and bioaccumulative impacts of chemical contaminants, and
- the lack of provision for regular health surveys.

Throughout this intensive year-long debate, the owners of the landfill — York Sanitation, a subsidiary of Waste Management Inc. of Illinois — kept a low profile. The Ministry of the Environment fought the defense for the company while business went on as usual. Fran Sainsbury described the situation:

> The citizens have been going at it tooth and nail and bloodying the noses of the Ministry who really should be working for us. All the time that we are doing this and spending great energy and becoming tired doing it, York Sanitation is going to the bank happily every weekend with their bags of money.[74]

In April 1982, although still insisting that there was no real cause for concern, the Minister of the Environment announced that York Sanitation would be required to supply water to 12 residences around the landfill and to close down the dump by the end of June 1983. York Sanitation appealed the Minister's decision. In addition, the Ministry of Health allocated $1.3 million to conduct a health survey of the community.

The people of Whitchurch-Stouffville remained worried. A 1982 report from the Ministry of the Environment concluded: "The organic contents of the landfill site represent a potential hazard for future contamination, but based on the analytical data contained in this report, there is no indication that such contamination is occurring at the present time."[75] But water testing by HB & O Engineering Limited and two other labs already indicated contamination, and preliminary surveys done by the citizens' groups showed health problems. These results have not been disputed by the government.

What the future would bring was unknown. Fran Sutton expressed the resentment created by this situation: "Certain people had the rough luck to be situated beside a landfill. Are they expendable because of that?"[76]

CHAPTER FOUR
THE SEARCH FOR
NEW WASTE DISPOSAL FACILITIES

IN THE LATE 1960's, serious concerns about the long-term effects of indiscriminate dumping of hazardous wastes began to be raised in a concerted way by environmental groups, scientists, neighbours of waste disposal sites, and government. They all stressed the need for new and safe waste disposal facilities. One-and-a-half decades later, such facilities are rarely available. The Ontario Ministry of the Environment assessed the Canadian situation in late 1980:

> At present there are no appropriate facilities in Ontario or Canada for the treatment and disposal of hazardous wastes, and only inadequate facilities for treatment and disposal of liquid industrial wastes. Storage of hazardous wastes and improper disposal of large volumes of liquid industrial wastes present the very real threat of serious environmental contamination such as pollution of our water supply, which in turn can threaten the health and well being of all Ontario residents.[1]

The Private Sector

THE ONTARIO GOVERNMENT URGED private corporations to provide the facilities necessary for hazardous waste disposal. As the 1970's proceeded, however, it became evident that private enterprise was unable to meet this responsibility.

One by one, existing waste disposal operations were closed.[2] Pressure from the State of Michigan forced the Ontario government to ban the deep-welling of industrial wastes into a rock formation in Lambton County after contamination of subsurface brines over 100 miles away in Michigan was linked to the Ontario disposal wells. The last of these wells, one operated by Tricil, was closed at the end of 1976. An incinerator, built in the Hamilton area by Thermal Destruction Systems in 1973, was closed in 1977. Although there were numerous complaints about the environmental effects of the incinerator, the company's announced reason for the closing was that there were not sufficient wastes to support the three incinerators that were operating in Ontario at the time.

Another liquid waste incinerator, this one situated in Mississauga and owned by Tricil, was closed in July 1978 because of inadequate pollution control equipment. After serious concerns were raised about the experimental solidification process at the Upper Ottawa Street landfill in Hamilton, the facility was closed in April 1980. Evidence showed that the company had not been abiding by provincial government regulations.

At the same time that special facilities such as these were being closed, the safety of the most common method for disposing of liquid industrial wastes — landfills — was called into question. During the 1970's, as a result of public concern about evidence of groundwater and surface water contamination, landfills were restricted from receiving liquid industrial wastes. A major loss of disposal space occurred in April 1978 when the Beare Road landfill in Metropolitan Toronto was closed to liquid industrial wastes, eliminating the main outlet in the Toronto area for this kind of disposal. Admitting the inadequacy of using landfills, the Minister of the Environment announced in 1978 that he would prohibit the disposal of all untreated liquid industrial wastes into landfills as of December 1979.[3] This proved impossible since sufficient alternative facilities were not available. Substantial progress, however, was made towards achieving this goal. As of May 1979, 19 Ontario landfills were known to be receiving liquid industrial wastes; by the end of December 1981, this had been reduced to only eight.

Over this period, the U.S. government began pressuring the Ontario government to limit the quantity and types of hazardous wastes being shipped from Ontario into the U.S. for disposal.

As the situation became more pressing, the province continued to ask private companies to develop new facilities. Three proposals to construct deep-wells for disposing inorganic liquid wastes into the Cambrian Shield never achieved results: Tricil dropped its deep-well proposal for Lambton County citing marketing uncertainties as the reason; proposals for similar wells in North Gosfield Township, just south of Windsor, and at Canborough in Haldimand-Norfolk were dropped by the proposing companies because of public opposition. A physical-chemical treatment complex and landfill proposed for the Nanticoke area was rejected by the Ministry of the Environment after public hearings indicated inadequacies with the proposal. A 1978 application for a liquid waste solidification plant in Fort Erie was withdrawn by the applicant. Also, a proposal for converting the Ajax sewage treatment plant into a liquid waste facility was withdrawn by the Durham Regional government in 1980.

photos courtesy of Tricil Ltd.

Photos of the Tricil Ltd. transfer station in Mississauga, Ontario. The bottom photo shows the holding tanks where wastes are stored before being shipped to one of the Tricil disposal operations.

These failures put the provincial government into a serious bind. The dangers of improper disposal were becoming more and more evident, but private companies were not developing new safe disposal facilities.

Given this situation, the province decided that the only way facilities could be developed would be if the government provided financial incentives to private companies. In November 1979, the province announced that it would become the co-proponent with two private companies for the development of two solidification plants — one in Harwich Township and the other in Thorold.

The government stated that it would appear at the public hearings to support the private companies in their bids for approval. The province also agreed to underwrite the costs of the public hearings and to pay the costs of moving the solidified materials to another location should problems arise at the sites in the future. But considerable public opposition to the plans arose, and the province withdrew from its co-proponent status. Subsequently, each company announced that it was withdrawing its application.

The Minister of the Environment, Harry Parrott, said in 1978 that the province "would only consider getting involved in the waste disposal business as an operator if it became obvious private enterprise won't or can't do the job."[4] Upon the collapse of all efforts to get private companies to take responsibility for developing proper facilities, the provincial government was forced to try a different tack. Parrott announced in 1980, "We can and do fully accept the responsibility as a government for the operation of a [liquid industrial waste treatment facility and] site."[5]

The Ontario Waste Management Corporation

THE GOVERNMENT ANNOUNCED in November 1980 that 750 acres of land in South Cayuga were to become the location of a major industrial waste disposal facility owned and operated by the province. A crown corporation, the Ontario Waste Management Corporation (OWMC), was created to develop and operate this facility.

The people of South Cayuga viewed the decision to locate in their community as a political one and not an environmentally sound one. A consultant hired by the province to recommend sites had not even included in its first report the South Cayuga site as one of the potential locations for liquid waste disposal facilities.[6] The real reason for the choice of South Cayuga, people suspected, was that the government owned a substantial tract of land in the area.

Formed two weeks before Parrott's announcement, the Haldimand-Norfolk Organization for a Pure Environment (HOPE) mounted a boisterous and effective opposition to the disposal plant. At an information meeting in the Dunnville High School, an angry crowd of over 2,000 expressed their opinions of the government's decision. "The Conservative government doesn't have the guts to do what's right, just what's politically feasible," commented one resident.[7] "If the site is so safe," said another, "then submit it to an Environmental Assessment."[8] Ministry of the Environment officials refused to attend the meeting, abandoning the head of the Waste Management Corporation, Dr. Donald Chant, to face the crowd alone.

From almost the day of the announcement, HOPE gave clear technical reasons for questioning the suitability of the site. HOPE chairperson, Phil Hinman, outlined the group's concerns:

Our main concern is that it is on a floodplain. Secondly, gas wells have been in the area for nigh on to 100 years. The records of them are incomplete and we're afraid those wells tap straight into the aquifer. In addition, the area is close to the Grand River and we are concerned that material could get into the river. Dunnville's auxiliary drinking water is four miles down the Grand. We're also concerned about the transportation hazards.[9]

One year less seven days after the government's announcement of its plans for South Cayuga, the Ontario Waste Management Corporation abandoned the plan. The technical restrictions of the land — limitations that the South Cayuga residents had pointed out a year before — were too severe. Chant said, "The corporation would be unwise to contemplate locating a landfill on what was now acknowledged to be a marginal or borderline site."[10]

The government was back to square one. One year and an estimated $750,000 later,[11] the Ontario Waste Management Corporation had to start over.

The search for new waste disposal facilities had failed. As Ontario entered the mid-1980's neither private corporations nor the provincial government had succeeded in developing proper facilities.

The NIMBY Syndrome

BOTH PRIVATE CORPORATIONS and government blame the public for their failure to develop safe systems to handle hazardous wastes. It is because of a "not in my backyard" (NIMBY) syndrome, they claim, that facilities have not been developed. The following statement by Harry Parrott, Ontario's former Minister of the Environment, is typical:

> In our society we enjoy and require the benefits of industrial and chemical technology. We simply cannot expect to reap these benefits and at the same time refuse to accept responsibility for accommodating the wastes which are by-products of that technology.
>
> No one wants a liquid industrial waste facility, or for that matter any kind of disposal facility near or in his or her neighbourhood. There comes a time, however, when all but the most biased must accept that something must be done in the broader public interest and in accepting a degree of responsibility as a member of the community.
>
> Is it asking too much for citizens to accept a facility in their community because it's the best place for it and because the facility is required to serve the public's need in general?[12]

Farmers and townspeople who live next door to hazardous disposal practices are infuriated by statements such as these. When the Minister of the Environment accused the people of Harwich of refusing to accept their duty to society, they spoke out strongly:

> We are paying for them [the benefits of industry] and industry is
> making the profit. It's up to industry to get rid of their wastes at their
> expense, not ours.
>
> Don't sit me across the table and tell me it's my problem! I've paid
> for the profit. I'm willing to pay the extra price.
>
> It's the environment that's paying now and you can't replace the
> environment. When it's contaminated, the damage is done.
>
> A stop must be put to it! They've got to tell industry they can't
> produce the item if they don't know how to deal with the wastes.[13]

Industry responds to such statements by saying that wastes are
the by-product of consumer demand; therefore they are the responsibility of society as a whole and not that of the manufacturers of
waste. Production decisions are made in corporate boardrooms.
Before production begins, the costs of production, the available
technologies and the expected market demand are each carefully
assessed. If profit levels are projected to be high enough, production will proceed.

It is clear to all concerned that if there are no sales, there will be
no profit. Industry managers claim that the deciding factor is consumer demand, thereby putting the consuming public in the driver's seat when it comes to manufacturing decisions.

However, many studies show that consumer demand is not
necessarily the result of an individual's freedom of choice. Instead,
mechanisms like advertising allow corporate executives to significantly affect trends in the marketplace. One of the earlier descriptions of the conscious development of this demand was Vance Packard's 1957 book, *The Hidden Persuaders*. Packard quoted a Mil-
waukee advertising executive:

> "The cosmetic manufacturers are not selling lanolin, they are selling
> hope ... we no longer buy oranges, we buy vitality. We do not buy
> just an auto, we buy prestige."
>
> By 1957 American merchandising persuaders were embarked on
> several bold and portentious attempts to create new, broader, or
> more insatiable demands for their products.[14]

The campaign to create demand has continued unabated with
nearly four and a half billion dollars spent on advertising in 1981 in
Canada alone.

The desire to expand profits is the motivating factor behind
ever-increasing production and the concomitant increased wastes.
The only way to protect oneself from diminishing profits is to grow
constantly. As a result, growth — increased production and consumption — are primary corporate goals. The corporate quest for
profit — not consumer demand — is the driving force behind
growth.

The Record

GOVERNMENT AND INDUSTRY give the impression that the severe limitation upon where wastes can be disposed is a product of the NIMBY syndrome: the public simply will not allow facilities to be built. However, the record shows that the public has valid reasons for its resistance.

At the beginning of this chapter, it was indicated that four disposal facilities ended operations between 1976 and 1980. Each was closed because of the environmental and health problems it posed. The deep-well near Sarnia was closed because of complaints from the Michigan State government. The two incinerators were closed by the companies involved because they were not willing to make the expenditures required by the provincial government that would bring them up to proper safety standards. The solidification plant was closed because a leaking liner had allowed 270,000 gallons of chemical wastes to seep into the ground. In those instances where it may have been possible to make corrections to avoid future contamination of the environment, the owners of the operations were unwilling to make the expenditures required to keep the facilities operating. In some of these cases, local residents were instrumental in bringing problems to the attention of the Ministry of the Environment and making it clear how severely the facilities were endangering the environment.

Many landfills have lost the right to have liquid industrial wastes dumped into them. The Ministry announced as early as 1978 that it was unsafe to dump untreated liquid industrial wastes into landfills. One can hardly blame supposedly unreasonable neighbours for these closures.

Likewise, the record on proposals for new facilities does not support industry and government contentions that the NIMBY syndrome is making it impossible to deal with the hazardous wastes problem.

The three proposals for deep-wells in Ontario were dropped by the companies involved at very preliminary stages. Local people had the opportunity to ask only a few questions before the companies withdrew their proposals. If the companies had had faith in the ability of their proposals to withstand scrutiny, it is difficult to understand why they withdrew before it was evident that organized neighbourhood objections would arise.

The proposal for a 100-acre waste disposal site and treatment complex at Nanticoke was turned down when Ministry officials decided that the company had not given adequate assurance that it could control liquids leaking from the site and provide protection against spills or breakdowns. No guarantees were given that an acceptable quality of effluent from the proposed treatment facility into the Nanticoke Creek could be achieved.[15]

These concerns came out at the public hearings under pressure from concerned residents in the area. Joe Castrilli of the Canadian Environmental Law Association said:

> The Nanticoke hearing itself raised important questions as to the wisdom of leaving it all to the government experts. Intervenors pointed out, for example, that 1) the MOE often accepted data and figures from the applicant without inquiring into the validity; 2) that despite its support for the use of plastic liners, MOE in fact had neither the experience nor the expertise with them; and 3) that although normal MOE responsibilities include thorough investigation of proposals before recommending them for hearing, it was only during the hearings themselves that MOE admitted that if it had known about a local community water intake pipe it would not have recommended Nanticoke Creek as a discharge point.[16]

In 1979, the Regional Municipality of Durham with the support of the Ministry of the Environment decided to convert an unused sewage treatment plant into a facility for treating 8.8 million gallons yearly of liquid wastes. After 38 days of public hearings spread over six months, the hearing panel recommended against proceeding with the facility. Finally, the Regional Municipality withdrew its application.

In their presentations before the Environmental Assessment Board, Ajax Citizens Together presented evidence of technical problems that had not been given adequate attention by the Regional Municipality and the Ministry of the Environment. Among the important omissions in the proposal were: consideration of impacts on adjacent residences, on recreational lands and on the Duffin Creek ecosystem; consideration of the on-site soil and groundwater conditions, the location of the facility on a floodplain and the plans for disposal of the treated wastes that the facility would generate.[17]

In the cases of the two solidification plant proposals, the provincial government withdrew its support in favour of a more grandiose scheme at South Cayuga. The two companies involved in the projects dropped out before the hearing stage had been reached. Considerable public opposition had developed in both of these communities before the government and the companies withdrew. It had become clear that substantial evidence would be presented at public hearings by those opposed to the project. At the time of the withdrawal by the government, a spokesperson for the Ministry of the Environment lamented:

> The concern we've got is that they [the citizens] have made the verdict before the [assessment] process has been allowed to work. They don't seem to wish to proceed through an assessment.[18]

But it was the government and companies that chose not to proceed with an assessment.

The province's plan for South Cayuga also ended in withdrawal. The Grand River's floodplain, the presence of gas wells, and the shallow covering of clay over much of the area had been pointed out earlier as limitations to the site by residents. These were confirmed by government studies as was the presence of drumlins whose rocky content would provide easy and quick access for leachate to the bedrock and the groundwater.

The Ministry of the Environment and private companies complain that the public's negative reactions to their proposals have interfered with efforts to find a reasonable solution to the hazardous waste problem. This complaint is contradicted by the record. Public input has had a major impact on decisions, but those who have reviewed the record insist that the public's input has always resulted in rejections on significant grounds. According to Joe Castrilli, "While the issue is certainly an emotional one, recent industry proposals in Ontario have been rejected because they were found wanting on technical grounds — not emotional grounds."[19] These inadequacies may not have been discovered until it was too late without the vigilance of citizens concerned about protecting their environment.

In each recent proposal for liquid industrial waste disposal facilities, serious flaws have been found, and the project has been halted. The positive impact of citizen participation is clearest in the case of landfills that are being designated for municipal and solid industrial wastes. Evidence has consistently come out at public hearings that has resulted in better controls being placed upon the landfill operation than might otherwise have been the case. The Glanbrook landfill is just one example.

At 58 sessions before the Environmental Assessment Board, the Binbrook Anti-Dump Committee and the Chippawa Watershed Association presented evidence pointing out the flaws in the landfill proposed by the Regional Municipality of Hamilton-Wentworth. As a result of these hearings, the Board recommended and the Ministry accepted 13 conditions for the operation of the site that had not been originally built into the proposal. These included moving the boundaries back from the flood plain and developing a plan for leachate removal. The Regional Municipality made these refinements. Recognizing the value of public input, the Township appointed three members of the Binbrook Anti-Dump Committee to sit on its landfill advisory committee.

Dr. Ed Farkas, a professor of environmental studies at the University of Waterloo, said that public participation such as that at Glanbrook has positive consequences:

> Twenty years from now the Ontario government may be very grateful that citizen intervention pointed out the need for changes. Without these changes, waste management operations at the site may have resulted in severe environmental contamination problems, requiring large expenditures of money to correct.[20]

Governments and private companies involved in the waste management business have come to realize that opposition to waste disposal facilities will inevitably arise. In the past both government and private companies tried to deal with such opposition by acting secretively. This tactic proved disastrous. The public reacted with hostility, which frequently led to irreconcilable differences between the community and the company. For government, the secretive approach meant that proposals were allowed to proceed without being fully examined. Only when brought into the bright sunshine of public scrutiny do the full implications and the real limitations of proposals become known. As a result of this secretive approach, many long-term negative impacts upon the welfare of communities and the environment were ignored, and public distrust of government officials has grown.

After experiences like this, both government and private companies now speak of the need to involve the public in the process. While many still resist the notion that public participation is justifiable or necessary, they have at least become aware of the fact that it must be dealt with. From the perspective of industry, this awareness usually means attempting to soothe public concern by "educating the public about the necessity of proper disposal and the environmental safety of the properly operated disposal sites."[21] Companies expect governments to undertake much of this educating process. In turn, a government often requires a company to hold information sessions at which the public can ask questions about the proposal.

Government representatives understand that education alone is not the answer. Experience has led them to conclude that "the problem is not so much one of technology but primarily a social problem of location of disposal sites,"[22] and that the public must feel that they are part of the decision-making process. It has become a well established practice that public hearings be held to allow people to express their concerns in a formal way and to cross-examine company and government witnesses.

Governments have viewed waste disposal siting as a "public relations" problem. To this end, studies are made to find techniques for gaining public acceptance of waste disposal projects. These studies are aimed at finding a solution to what is considered by the government to be a kneejerk "not in my backyard" reaction. The U.S. Environmental Protection Agency study entitled "Siting of Hazardous Waste Management Facilities and Public Opposition" begins:

> The major conclusion of this study is that public opposition ... is the most critical problem in developing new facilities .... Overcoming this opposition will require diligence and imagination.[23]

All these studies have as their motivating force the desire to overcome or moderate public opposition — rather than to find the safest and best solution possible. The necessity for, and legitimacy of, public input in order to arrive at the best solution to the problem of hazardous waste disposal is rarely accepted by government and corporate officials. Instead, it is seen as an obstacle to be overcome rather than a vital part of a democratic process. Public input is accepted as necessary only to avoid getting into trouble with community residents.

CHAPTER FIVE
THE DECISION-MAKING PROCESS

DESPITE THE FORCES working against it, the idea of public input into decision-making about waste disposal has been forged into some actual channels. Legislation has been enacted in Ontario to formalize the process of public input into waste decisions.

Opportunities for Public Input

ACCORDING TO ONTARIO'S *Environmental Protection Act*, public hearings must be held on applications for hauled liquid industrial waste or hazardous waste disposal sites. On applications for treatment facilities that do not actually include disposal, the hearing is optional, but hearings are normally held in such cases as well. Public hearings are not conducted on applications for certificates of approval to transport wastes. Table 6 describes the process that must be gone through before a permit can be obtained to operate a waste disposal facility.

A three-person panel chosen from the Environmental Assessment Board conducts the public hearings. The members of the Board are appointed by the Lieutenant-Governor in Council (the Cabinet). Each party to the hearing has the opportunity to call witnesses and to cross-examine each other's witnesses.

The main opportunity for citizen input is at this stage. Citizens' groups devote considerable energy to preparation for and participation in these hearings, yet those who have gone through the process often remain doubtful about the usefulness of the energy they expend.

Ontario has two pieces of legislation under which approvals for projects that may affect the environment can be considered: the *Environmental Protection Act* and the *Environmental Assessment Act*. With the exception of Harwich and Thorold, neither of which reached the hearing stage, the Ministry of the Environment has considered proposals for waste disposal sites under the *Environmental Protection Act*. The public has constantly pressed for wider use of the *Environmental Assessment Act*. This Act requires that the potential environmental impacts of a project be looked at from a

Table 6
Steps in the Approval Process
Under Ontario's Environmental Protection Act

No one may operate or alter a waste management system or a waste disposal site in Ontario without a certificate of approval from the provincial Ministry of the Environment. This requirement includes landfills, incinerators, solidification plants, the transportation of wastes and any other method of disposal. Recycling and reclamation projects do not require this approval.

Step 1: Application for certificate of approval to the Director of Approvals, Ministry of the Environment.

Step 2: Discussions between the applicant and the Ministry.

Step 3: Public hearings before the Environmental Assessment Board except in applications to transport waste.

Step 4: Recommendation of the Environmental Assessment Board to the Director of Approvals except on matters of waste transportation.

Step 5: Decision of the Director of Approvals.

Step 6: Possible appeal of Director's decision by the applicant to the Environmental Appeal Board within 15 days.

Step 7: Possible appeal of Board's decision by any party to the hearing to the Minister of the Environment within 30 days.

wider perspective than under the *Protection Act*. The *Assessment Act* includes as part of its definition of the environment "social, economic, and cultural considerations that influence the life of man or a community." In addition, the need for the project must be proven and alternative means of filling the need must be carefully assessed.

Because of this wider range of considerations, the time involved in preparing for and conducting hearings under the *Environmental Assessment Act* would usually be longer than under the *Environmental Protection Act*. In 1980 then Minister of the Environment, Harry Parrott, explained why there would not be an *Environmental Assessment Act* hearing in the consideration of its South Cayuga proposal. The time for such a hearing, he claimed, could not be afforded. "I make no apologies whatsoever for attacking what is one of the most serious problems in this province and getting on with the job."[1] However, many of the citizens in those neighbourhoods where such sites are being proposed feel that, with such potentially damaging intrusions into their communities, no adequate justification is possible for curtailing the evaluation procedures. A common sentiment in South Cayuga after the Minister's announcement was, "If the Minister is so proud and feels the plan is so foolproof, he should have no fear of going to an environmental hearing."[2]

Indeed, it is the citizens' groups whose resources are strained by the time needed for public hearings. The hearings themselves take up 30 or 40 days spread over two to three months. As well, considerable time is required to prepare for the hearings. This makes them a fulltime job for those involved, placing a substantial burden on volunteer organizations. According to Sheila May, who attended 58 days of hearings on the Glanbrook landfill site on behalf of the Binbrook Anti-Dump Committee in 1979, "The biggest problem is the amount of time that you have to sustain the energy for."[3] The issues involved, however, are so critical to these communities that there have always been people willing to make this sacrifice.

Another problem with the Environmental Assessment Board hearings is the lack of evening sessions. A mothers' group in Whitchurch-Stouffville became frustrated because neither they nor their husbands could attend the daytime hearings of the Environmental Assessment Board during the spring of 1981. One afternoon, the mothers walked into the hearing room with their children and sat down. This, naturally enough, created more than the usual amount of noise. "It was getting rather difficult to conduct the hearings," admitted one of the mothers.[4] They refused to leave until a date had been set for an evening meeting. After some confusion and a hurried checking of date books, the hearing panel set such a date. The mothers and their children left.

It has become normal practice for the Environmental Assessment Board to hold one evening meeting during its hearings in order to allow people from a broader spectrum of the community to express their concerns about a proposed waste disposal site. However, attending a single meeting is only a partial form of participation in the hearing process.

Frequently, technical matters are the focal point at public hearings. Therefore, citizens' groups need technical experts to appear on their behalf and to prepare them to cross-examine the other parties' experts. Local residents also need legal advice; it is useful to have a lawyer present through the entire proceedings. Technical experts and lawyers are extremely costly. Citizens' groups have asked the government for funding to help them prepare and conduct their cases, but the government has always refused. The three and one-half months of hearings in 1981 over a landfill site in Harwich Township cost $10,000 for the citizens' group, Citizens Rebel-

photo: Marg McArthur

photo: John Jackson

Top photo: Lillian Tomen, CRAW chairperson (centre) at CRAW demonstration, 9 August 1980.
Bottom photo: CRAW blockade at the Ridge Landfill, January 1981.

ling Against Waste. The Concerned Citizens of Whitchurch-Stouffville estimated that they had to raise $15,000 to cover their costs of preparing for and appearing at the appeal initiated by Waste Management Inc. in 1982.

In two instances, the government promised financial support to the applicants, but refused assistance to the local residents. In 1979, Browning-Ferris Industries Ltd. and Walker Brothers applied to the Ministry of the Environment to build solidification plants in Harwich Township and in Thorold. The Ministry promised that, if the proposals were rejected, the government would pay them up to a maximum of *$100,000* each towards their preparation costs for the public hearings. Despite the concerted efforts of the citizens' groups in those areas to get funding to help them prepare their cases, the Ministry refused. As a result, BFI, the largest waste disposal company in North America, and Walker Brothers, a subsidiary of SCM Corporation, were given government funds to prepare for the hearings while the local residents were left to scrounge money through bake sales, selling bumper stickers, and the solicitation of donations from local service clubs and supporters.

It should be no surprise that citizens' experiences have made them sceptical of Ontario's public hearing process. Many suspect the hearings are a charade whose outcome is preordained. The people of Whitchurch-Stouffville went through two sets of Environmental Assessment Board hearings over the landfill in their community. Fran Sainsbury, who worked on both the 1974 and the 1981 hearings, described her conclusions from that experience:

> The first time around we were very unsophisticated. We honestly thought that this was a legal process. You stood up and you gave your technical evidence. We felt we really had it in the bag. We thought at that time, all you had to do was tell it like it is. We didn't realize that the central region of the Ministry of the Environment is so deeply engrossed in landfill itself. They work hand-in-glove with the people from those companies. They are very involved with industry.[5]

After the public hearings, the Environmental Assessment Board makes a recommendation to the Ministry's Director of Approvals as to whether the proposed facility should be accepted. The entire Environmental Assessment Board, not just the three members attending the hearings, make the recommendations.

In one known instance, the report of the whole Board directly contradicted the recommendations of those who attended the hearings. Durham Regional Council had proposed the conversion of an unused sewage treatment plant into a liquid waste treatment facility. All three members of the Environmental Assessment Board who attended the hearings urged the Board to recommend rejection of the proposal. They said the site was too close to homes and recreational lands; they were also concerned that flooding would present serious problems. Despite this urging, the majority of the members on the 16-person Board overrode their objections and recommended approval of the project. The people who heard the citizens' input were not the ones who made the final recommendation. The frustrated chairman of the hearing panel resigned. A representative of the citizens' group described the impact of this situation:

The EAB not only lost a well-respected, well-liked and intelligent member with the resignation of Keith Laver [the chairman of the Ajax hearing panel]; it also lost a large part of its reputation for integrity and political independence.[6]

Ultimately the Regional Council withdrew its application, but regardless of the final outcome, a major flaw in the system had been demonstrated.

The Environmental Assessment Board is the only group that hears directly the concerns and evidence of the public, but it is not the body that makes the decision. The decision is made by the Director of Approvals, a civil servant who does not attend the public hearings.

The Director of Approvals treats the Environmental Assessment Board's report as only one of several inputs. He also bases his decision on the comments of Ministry staff, both those who work in Toronto and in the region where the project is to be built. Ministry people generally have had considerable contact with the proponent for the project, and little contact with the citizens. In evidence before the Environmental Assessment Board in 1979, the District Officer of the Ministry of the Environment in the Hamilton region described this interaction:

> It was necessary to work very closely with the applicant. Correspondence and meetings prior to the Hearing attempted to resolve outstanding questions related to problem areas. Mr. Hicks [the Ministry officer] stated that the purpose of one meeting was to review with the Region [the applicant] the future strategy needed in order to adequately prepare for the Environmental Assessment Board hearings, and to request further explanation or detail on several points.[7]

This communication is normal practice.

The Director of Approvals is isolated from the public not only because he does not attend the hearings, but also because he is not politically accountable. In his report on waste management practices in Maple and Whitchurch-Stouffville, Judge Hughes dwelt upon this unusual aspect of the Director of Approval's position:

> That decision [the issuing of a certificate of approval] may be taken without reference to his superiors or to the Minister who has to answer for his conduct in the Legislative Assembly. I venture to say, with some knowledge of both the provincial and federal civil services, that this procedure is unique in both principle and practice and relieves the elected head of the Ministry not only of important powers but of awkward responsibilities.[8]

Another source of frustration is the lack of a right to appeal the

Director's decision. Only the person who applied to build the disposal facility can make such an appeal.

In April 1982, the Director of Approvals rejected an application by Waste Management of Canada Ltd. for continuation and expansion of its landfill site at Whitchurch-Stouffville. The company promptly appealed the decision and was given the opportunity to re-present its arguments. In 1976, when an earlier request for expansion of the same site had been approved by the Ministry, the local residents had had no right of appeal. John Swaigen, a lawyer with the Canadian Environmental Law Association, represented the Whitchurch-Stouffville citizens at the earlier hearings. After the 1976 decision, he concluded:

> Only by offsetting the applicant's right of appeal with a similar right of appeal for opponents, and offsetting the applicant's ability to negotiate with a similar right for opponents to negotiate, can people such as my clients be assured of proper environmental protection and of proper consideration for recommendations made by the Environmental Hearing Board [now called Environmental Assessment Board]. This one-sided appeal process and negotiation process offends any concept of fairness.[9]

The public's access to the courts to challenge waste disposal decisions is quite limited. Legal arguments can only be made on the basis of failure to follow proper procedure. Even in these cases, the provincial government has sometimes argued that the court has no jurisdiction and has at least once allowed a company to ignore a court decision.

The people of Harwich Township believed that Browning-Ferris Industries did not have a valid certificate of approval for the Ridge Landfill site. In 1980, the Township Council took BFI to court in an effort to determine the validity of the certificate. The Supreme Court of Ontario ruled in December of that year that the site was not properly licensed to receive liquid industrial wastes. Despite the ruling, officials from the Ministry of the Environment told BFI it could continue to dump liquid wastes into the landfill.

The Harwich citizens were stunned by the Ministry's action. One freezing January morning in 1981, they decided to protect their community. Several members of Citizens Rebelling Against Waste put their farm tractors in front of the landfill's gates, blocking all traffic. When asked by the police to leave, they refused. The business, they said, was not lawful; they pointed out to the police that the courts had ruled that BFI did not have a legal certificate of approval. They maintained the blockade for three days. When an injunction was issued and the courts promised to re-hear the case, the farmers removed their tractors.

The Ontario Divisional Court ruled a year later that the portion of the certificate that permitted liquid industrial wastes and hazardous wastes to be dumped was invalid because a public hearing had not been held. It ordered an end to the dumping of these substances. This time the Ministry did not interfere with the court's decision. Liquid industrial wastes and hazardous wastes were no longer dumped into the Harwich landfill after November 1981.

The court's decision had broader ramifications, calling into question the legality of dumping liquid industrial wastes at eight other landfills in Ontario. The Minister of the Environment, Keith Norton, took immediate action. He stated,

> We cannot afford to risk the loss of facilities essential for the disposal of these liquid industrial wastes pending such time as an alternative treatment and disposal facility is established and in operation.[10]

The Ontario Cabinet immediately issued an order-in-council stating that these eight landfills could continue to accept liquid industrial wastes even if public hearings had not been conducted. This order was put into effect for five years.

Public Input and the OWMC

IN NOVEMBER 1980, a new element was introduced into the process for developing waste disposal facilities in Ontario. A government agency — the Ontario Waste Management Corporation (OWMC) — was made responsible for establishing a waste management system.

Recognizing the tarnished reputations that both the Ministry of the Environment and the waste disposal industry had among the public, the members of the Corporation went out of their way to emphasize that this was a new start, unconnected to the errors of the past. The chairman, Dr. Donald Chant, described what the OWMC would do in Ontario: "There is as yet no place on earth like it."[11] The Corporation would set an example for the rest of the world, he claimed, in both the use of the most technologically advanced waste management systems and in the most thorough public consultation programmes.

"Never again can we afford to arrive on community doorsteps unannounced," said Chant.[12] To this end, the Corporation undertook a public information and public input programme. One of their news releases said:

> OWMC is committed to involving the public as it moves through each stage of the site selection process. Most importantly, we want this

process to be an open one, where all sides are benefiting from shared information, and where concerned citizens and organized groups have an opportunity to express their views before decisions are made.[13]

This early involvement of the public was a break from past practices where corporations developed their proposals in private, and the public was not involved in the preliminary discussions between the government and the proponent.

The public, however, was not guaranteed the right to public hearings, as the Corporation's proposals were exempted from the hearings requirements of both the *Environmental Assessment Act* and the *Environmental Protection Act*.

At a meeting in August 1982 between citizens' groups and the Minister of the Environment, Norton asserted, "There is no chance that existing legislation exempting the Ontario Waste Management Corporation from the *Environmental Assessment Act* will be appealed."[14]

The provincial cabinet must appoint a committee to review the Corporation's proposals and make a report to the cabinet. It is likely, as was true in South Cayuga, that this review committee will conduct public hearings. However, the topics to be discussed, the timing and length of the hearings are at the discretion of the cabinet and the review panel.

Consultation with the public by the proponent for facilities is a significant step forward. This consultation is not, however, guaranteed by the legislation setting up the Corporation. A change in board membership could bring a change in consultation policies. Consultation also does not replace the need to have a body other than the proponent conduct a thorough public assessment. When the OWMC is the proponent, such hearings and their procedures are at the discretion of the cabinet. The public has no control of the format of those hearings.

The legislation setting up the OWMC directed the Corporation to locate a facility in South Cayuga. Even though this site was rejected, the Corporation cannot go elsewhere until an order-in-council is passed by the provincial cabinet stating that another specific site may be used. Such an order-in-council could come at the initiative of the board of directors of the OWMC or the Minister of the Environment.

Once a site is designated the Corporation may not proceed unless studies show that "the property is a safe place for the facility and that the proposal for the facility is technologically sound."[15]

Since the crown corporation is obliged to follow the policies formulated by the cabinet, this means that the Corporation can stop a proposal of the cabinet only because of safety problems. If the Corporation does not want to proceed with a proposal for other than safety-related reasons, it could be obliged to proceed anyway. The site might be considered undesirable because of its impact on a community's planned development. The presence of a huge waste disposal plant might be economically harmful to the community, diminishing its tourist and recreation potential. This would not be considered a safety concern and thus not grounds for the OWMC to stop development. The proposal would be stopped only if the cabinet were dissuaded by the Corporation or, more likely, by public pressure.

Although this crown corporation has made a serious attempt to get public input, there are no legislative guarantees that the public will have more access to the decision-making processes than in the past.

The government's lack of commitment to the public hearings aspect of the approvals process for waste disposal facilities has become quite obvious. The government refuses to use the more thorough public hearing provisions of the *Environmental Assessment Act*. It quickly passed a special regulation exempting existing landfills from possible court challenges because they had not had public hearings. It passed a regulation removing the automatic five-year review for existing facilities — a review that required public hearings. And in the case of its own crown agency, it exempted its proposals for new facilities from the public hearings guarantees of both the *Environmental Assessment Act* and the *Environmental Protection Act*.

The government explains its limiting of public input by pointing to the urgency of the problem and the necessity of streamlining the process. It claims the public is the cause of the delays. During debate in the Ontario Legislature, Parrott was blunt about this:

> Quite frankly, the controversy surrounding each proposal has meant it has taken too long to implement what I am sure everyone agrees is a legitimate objective.[16]

But the valuable contribution made by the public in the past points out the dangers of not allowing full public input. Too often it is forgotten that the real problem is the hazardous wastes — not the public. The public provides a central part of the method for reaching a solution.

CHAPTER SIX
TOWARDS A NEW
WASTE MANAGEMENT SYSTEM

ONTARIO'S PROVINCIAL GOVERNMENT, like most governments, has been hoping to develop new and safe facilities to deal with the escalating problems created by hazardous wastes. However, its efforts have been unsuccessful because of a major strategic flaw. The search by government and industry has focused upon building new disposal facilities and finding new technologies for containing and destroying waste. This strategy ignores many other available methods that can be used to protect the environment from the perils that are created by hazardous wastes. Rather than a new waste *disposal* system, a new waste *management* system should be the focus of this search. This chapter describes the components of such a waste management system.

The Principles

MASSIVE RAW MATERIAL inputs and cheap waste disposal techniques are two pillars upon which the current system of production is based. But natural resources are not infinite and cheap disposal is not the most effective waste management system. Each of these pillars is now beginning to crumble, threatening the whole structure with collapse.

The beliefs in limitless raw materials and in cheap waste disposal have reinforced each other in a psychology of perpetual growth. They are used as an argument against recycling methods which necessitate greater investment but maximize the use of materials. Consequently, waste and risks to the environment continue to mount. In addition, careless waste disposal techniques have directly contributed to the diminishing availability of resources. The *Global 2000 Report* to the U.S. President in 1981 pointed out that even renewable resources are in danger of running out. "These resources are renewable *if* they are kept in a condition of health. But they are susceptible to disruption, contamination, and destruction."[1] Disposal of hazardous wastes in negligent ways is a substantial contributor to the loss of renewable resources.

In devising their strategies for handling wastes, it makes sense for both government and industry to use two paramount principles in judging the effectiveness of a waste management system: minimizing contamination of the environment and making the most efficient use of the earth's limited resources. These principles can be most effectively met by making waste management part of the original production plans.

The following would be the logical steps for a company to go through in developing its waste management programme.

Step 1: Describe the waste stream. Each waste stream has different characteristics which require particular management techniques.

Step 2: Reduce the waste quantities. For example, has there been maximum avoidance of spills and leakages?

Step 3: Recycle and reclaim wastes. Has there been all possible reuse of materials?

Step 4: Exchange wastes. Are there other companies that could use the wastes as materials for their production?

Step 5: Dispose of wastes. If there are still wastes left after maximum use of steps 2, 3 and 4, what are the safest ways available to dispose of the remainder?

Step 6: Substitute. If there is no safe way to dispose of a hazardous material, is there a safer material that could be used instead in the production process? or is it necessary not to produce the item at all in order to avoid serious harm to the environment and people's health?

Reduction of Wastes

THE IDEAL WASTE MANAGEMENT OPTION is to minimize the quantity of wastes. Numerous straightforward methods exist for achieving this goal. Simple housekeeping practices can have a surprisingly large impact on waste reduction. Avoiding spills and leaks as well as carefully retrieving and reusing the chemicals that do spill rather than carelessly turning them into wastes can be important. Mixing hazardous wastes with relatively harmless wastes can contaminate a much larger waste stream, magnifying the disposal problem.

Efficiently operating machinery can greatly reduce the quantity of wastes. For example, distillation residues from pesticide production contain dangerous pesticides and other toxic by-products. The California Office of Appropriate Technology has said these wastes can be reduced "by increasing the efficiency of distillation processes through equipment modification and careful process control."[2] The 3M Company of Minnesota reduced its annual pollution burden by "75,000 tons of air pollutants, 1325 tons of water pollutants, 500 million gallons of polluted wastewater and 2900 tons of sludge."[3] These dramatic reductions were achieved through process changes that guard against evaporation of chemicals, prevent leaks and avoid unnecessary use of materials. In addition to reducing wastes, these modifications lessened the quantities of materials that 3M had to purchase to produce a given quantity of goods. According to Pollution Probe, "Good housekeeping and other non-capital intensive fine-tuning measures can be expected to cut industrial wastes by as much as ten percent, almost immediately"[4]

Recycling and Reclamation

ONCE WAYS OF REDUCING the volume of wastes have been explored, methods for recycling and reclaiming wastes should be examined. Many production processes can be operated in a closed loop system; potential wastes are recycled for reuse within the plant. In other instances, reclamation can occur; valuable commodities are extracted from the waste stream and reused with the remainder of the waste stream being discarded.

The *Toronto Star* installed an ink recycler in 1978. Pollution Probe, a Toronto environmental group, described the impacts of this recycling operation:

> In the first eight months of operation, the *Star*'s $28,000 system cut disposal costs to zero and produced enough recycled ink to replace $40,000 of new ink.
>
> In addition, filtered ink is often better than new ink received from manufacturers. The recycling process produces an ink with smoother flow properties, better absorbency, faster drying characteristics and more uniform particle size.
>
> The *Star* runs the ink reclaimer two or three times a week. From May 18, 1978 to January 1979 over 260,000 pounds of waste ink were recovered, replacing new ink costing over 15 cents per pound.
>
> The Star no longer has to dispose of any ink.[5]

Some of the most hazardous waste streams have been greatly reduced by utilizing closed loop systems. Cyanides, for example, which are widely used in the plating industry, can have serious environmental impacts if disposed of improperly. However, the California Office of Appropriate Technology reported:

> Electroplating processes can be designed as closed-loop systems (producing no hazardous wastes for disposal) by incorporating process modifications to reduce rinse water volumes and by using separation processes such as evaporation, ion exchange, membrane techniques (reverse osmosis, electrodialysis), and electrolytic techniques to recover metal cyanides for reuse in plating baths.[6]

Solvents are commonly used in industry. The potential for them to be recycled and reclaimed is tremendous. Many companies currently have solvent recovery techniques built into the production process while others ship their used solvents to commercial recyclers for cleaning. Often the purified solvents are sold back to the company that originally supplied the solvent to the recycler. A number of commercial solvent recovery facilities are in operation in Ontario.

Examples abound of companies that have successfully reduced both their waste volumes and the quantity of materials they must use in production by installing closed loop production processes and in-plant recycling of material formerly considered waste.

Waste Exchange

WASTE MATERIALS cannot always be reused within the plant. This does not mean, however, that the material is useless. Waste from one company may be useful to another. Waste exchanges can turn wastes into valuable commodities by making sure they are transferred to a company that can use them.

Zero Waste Systems of California specializes in finding uses for waste products. Company president Paul Palmer says they provide an individualized service to their clients aimed at having companies produce "reusable byproducts instead of garbage".[7] They analyse the company's waste stream, develop a recycling strategy, process the chemical wastes or arrange for their processing, and market the final materials.

This kind of active waste exchange and transfer is unusual. The more widely used method for finding outlets is through listing wastes in a catalogue referred to as a waste exchange. The list is circulated and potential users of a particular waste contact the exchange which puts the two parties into contact with each other. The two companies then arrange the transfer of wastes. One major waste exchange has been established in Canada, operated by the Ontario Research Foundation.

Several European waste exchanges are highly successful, operating at about 30 to 40 percent efficiency.[8] The efficiency is calculated by comparing the number of exchanges with the number of items listed. Generally only a 10 percent success rate has been achieved in the U.S.; the Canadian Waste Exchange reports an even lower success ratio.[9]

Waste exchanges could have a significant impact in reducing the waste disposal problem. The California Office of Appropriate Technology reported that up to 95 percent of pharmaceutical wastes, 25 percent of organic chemical wastes, 40 percent of petro-leum refining wastes, 40 percent of paint and allied product wastes and 20 percent of small industrial machining operation wastes have the potential to be exchanged.[10] More active waste exchanges that require companies to list their wastes and then attempt to find outlets for them could increase the use of this method of waste reduction.

These three methods of dealing with wastes — reduction, recycling and waste exchange — most completely achieve the two goals set out for this waste management system. To the extent that they are successfully applied, the need to dispose of wastes is removed, and, consequently, potential dangers to the environment and to people's health from the disposal of hazardous wastes are eliminated. In addition, maximum use is made of materials and efficient use of resources is achieved.

Not all wastes can be handled through these three methods. Inevitably some by-products of the production process that are not useful will remain and must truly be classed as wastes. Many experts say, however, that a serious reduction, recycling and exchange programme could reduce wastes by 40 percent. Some experts in the field cite even more optimistic possibilities, some going as high as 80 percent.[11] Regardless of the range in their estimates, all agree that the impacts of these programmes could be substantial.

Disposal of Wastes

MANY METHODS EXIST for disposing of wastes.[12] These methods can be used singly or in combination to reduce both the quantity and the hazards of the wastes.

I: Physical, Chemical and Biological Treatment

Physical, chemical, and biological methods can detoxify waste materials, reduce the volume of waste or separate the hazardous from the non-hazardous components. These three methods are fre-quently used in combination.

Usually, the initial step is to use physical means to separate solids from liquids or to separate two liquids of differing densities. The principal methods for achieving separation, one of the simplest and most inexpensive treatments operations, are 1) sedimentation or settling, 2) flotation, 3) filtration, 4) centrifugation, 5) screening and 6) adsorption.

In the sedimentation process, wastes are placed in tanks or ponds where the heavier materials settle to the bottom because of the pull of gravity. For materials that do not easily settle out, a special precipitating agent can be added to encourage the process. For example, if allowed to settle, oily water will separate into oil and water, much like the separation of salad dressings when left for a long time. Once separated, the two new waste streams can be individually treated in the most suitable manner.

Flotation achieves the separation of materials by pushing bubbles up through the liquid waste. The tiny bubbles attach themselves to solid particles and float them to the surface where the particles can be gathered. This system is especially effective for light solids and greases.

A filtering medium can be used to remove solid materials or to filter water from sludges. A common filtration method is the pumping of waste water through a bed of sand or coal. Filter presses or rotary vacuum filtration can also be used to remove water from sludge.

Some solids and liquids are most effectively separated by rapidly rotating them inside a container known as a centrifuge. The solid materials collect against the inside wall of the centrifuge from which they can be collected. This process is called centrifugation.

In the screening process, the liquid waste stream is passed through a screen filter where the solid materials are collected.

Dilute amounts of organic material can often be separated from waste water by adsorption. Waste water is trickled over a highly porous surface, for example, activated carbon, and the organic material is bound to its surface. A fish tank filter is a scaled down version of the chemical adsorption process. When the surface of the adsorbing material has been saturated, it can no longer extract organics. It must then be replaced or cleaned.

The adsorption technique has proven highly effective in removing organics from a number of commercial waste water streams. A 99 percent removal rate has been found for PCBs and pesticides such as aldrin, dieldrin and DDT. Phenols have also been removed at a greater than 99 percent efficiency rate. Some inorganic substances, such as cyanide and chromium, have also been removed by adsorption systems. The U.S. Environmental Protection Agency is so convinced of the effectiveness of this technology for removing organic contaminants that it has recommended that municipalities use activated carbon adsorption systems in their drinking water treatment plants.

Physical treatment is only a preliminary part of the complete treatment programme. Usually both of the waste streams created by separation will require further treatment. In some instances, particularly after the adsorption process, it is possible that the one stream — water — can be returned to the environment without further treatment. In some cases, one of the waste streams or both can be recycled to become a useful material rather than being sent for further treatment.

In chemical treatment, chemicals are added to wastes to alter their nature. The objective is to make the waste less hazardous or to separate out specific components. Neutralization, precipitation, and oxidation/reduction are the most commonly used chemical treatment technologies.

Wastes with high acidity (low pH) are very corrosive and present a significant danger to human health and the environment. Highly alkaline wastes (high pH) are extremely caustic and also present dangers. These two hazards can be reduced by neutralization. In some cases, acidic and alkaline waste streams can be combined to neutralize each other; in other cases a chemical agent is added to achieve the same effect. According to the California Office of Appropriate Technology, neutralization can be used in treating:

> ... sulphuric or hydrochloric pickle liquor from steel cleaning, alkaline or acidic metal plating wastes, spent acid catalysts, acid sludges, washwater from the petrochemical industry, and leather tanning wastes. Acid gases and mists from incineration or other processes may also be neutralized by passing them through a flow of alkaline liquid.[13]

For safety reasons, the exact chemical nature of the wastes intended for neutralization must be known. For example, adding acid to cyanide or sulfide-bearing wastes can result in the formation of hydrogen sulphide and hydrogen cyanide gases, each of which is deadly.

Dissolved materials can often be removed from liquid waste by precipitation. Heavy metals such as iron, copper, chromium, nickel and zinc can be removed in this manner. Precipitation is achieved either by adding chemicals to change the pH of the waste and so to create insoluble particles or by changing the temperature to decrease the solubility of dissolved materials. Physical solid/liquid separation methods must then be used to separate the precipitated substances.

A number of very toxic materials can be treated effectively by chemical oxidation/reduction techniques. Chemical reactions convert a toxic chemical into a simpler and less toxic one. For example, hazardous cyanide wastes can be changed into nitrogen and carbon dioxide, both harmless materials. Sulphur compounds, pesticides, phenols, aldehydes and aromatic hydrocarbons can be treated in a similar way. These wastes are usually only treated by the chemical oxidation process when in liquid form and when low concentrations of the contaminants exist.

Chemical treatment often detoxifies wastes to the extent that precautions no longer need to be taken in their handling. In some instances, it allows materials to be reused. In many others, however, it is only one part of a treatment process which requires still more treatment before the wastes can finally be disposed of.

Some industrial waste streams can be treated by biological methods based on the same principles as those used in sewage treatment plants and garden compost piles. Micro-organisms detoxify organic wastes by decomposing them into carbon dioxide, water, and other simple molecules. Activated sludge, trickling filters, aerated lagoons, anaerobic digestion systems (without oxygen present), and composters are used to encourage the biological processes. However, an article in *Technology Review* by Selim Senkan and Nancy Stauffer from the Massachusetts Institute of Technology pointed out the limitations of the biological methods of waste treatment:

> The compounds in the waste must be nontoxic to the micro-organisms. The wastes must contain some water: enzymes play a key role in the micro-organisms' degradation of wastes and enzymes require water for their activity. Soluble organics must be kept to a minimum as they can inhibit the enzymatic conversion process and are generally unaffected by biological treatment.[14]

Some of these problems can be overcome through prior treatment by physical or chemical methods.

Physical, chemical, and biological treatment methods are important components of the waste management system. Their use can greatly reduce the volume and hazard of many waste streams; some of their products, however, will require additional treatment. Other wastes cannot be treated by these methods; they require the use of different waste management options.

II: Thermal Destruction (Incineration)

Thermal destruction units can be used to reduce both the volume and toxicity of many organic wastes. Heat applied in thermal destruction units breaks down the wastes into less complex materials.

"Some people think incineration is the magic wand of hazardous waste management," said *Waste Age Magazine*. "Wave the wand

and the wastes disappear."[15] Unfortunately things are not so simple. Hazardous wastes are no exception to the fundamental law of physics which states that matter cannot be created or destroyed, but only transformed. California's Office of Appropriate Technology concluded, "There is greater concern about the potential environmental effects of incineration than most other alternative technologies."[16]

The major concern about thermal destruction is the air emissions it causes. Three types of air emissions are created: 1) particulate matter, 2) combustion products, and 3) uncombusted or partially combusted organic materials.

The particles or inorganic salts and ash that can be released during incineration vary in size from one micron (a human hair is about 100 microns thick) to the size of a large grain of sand. These particles can be lung irritants and can carry with them dangerous uncombusted organics. Installation of scrubbers, filters, and electrostatic precipitators can reduce or eliminate particulate emissions.

The combustion products of incineration include water, carbon dioxide, and certain gases that, when contacting water, form acids. The exact acid created depends on the waste burnt. Incineration of PCBs, for example, produces hydrogen chloride gas. This gas, converted into hydrochloric acid, is extremely harmful to plants. Sulphur dioxide, a major contributor to acid rain, can also be released into the air by an incinerator. Alkaline scrubber systems can effectively remove these hazardous combustion products.

In addition to these air emissions, uncombusted or partially combusted organic wastes may be released into the air during incineration. If not controlled, these emissions can present serious health hazards. Destruction of over 99.99 percent of many organic wastes can occur if sufficient heat is applied for a long enough period of time. According to Alan Serper, vice-president of Energy and Environmental Analysis Incorporated in Garden City, New York,[17] the temperatures needed for complete incineration vary widely. For example, PCBs in sewage sludge should be burnt at 425°C while ethylene tars require a temperature of 1760°C. The time the material must remain at this temperature also varies according to the organics being burnt. PCBs mixed in sewage sludge require 0.1 second while nitrogen-containing pesticides need 74 seconds. For effective operation, thermal destruction units should be equipped with a device that will automatically shut down the unit if the temperature is not hot enough.

After completion of combustion, non-organic ash will be left in the incinerator. This ash usually contains inorganic salts and hazardous heavy metal particles. With some wastes, the quantity of ash left after thermal destruction can be substantial. The burning of paint sludge, for example, leaves ash totalling as much as 50 percent of the original waste material. The ash must then be sent for disposal.

The ash wastes gathered from the scrubbers, filters, and precipitators must also be sent for special disposal.

The type of thermal destruction unit to be used on a particular waste stream, or whether this type of technology should be used at all depends on three characteristics of the waste:

1) Does it have organic content? If it does not, thermal destruction will have no significant effect.

2) What are the inorganic materials that are in the waste? It is desirable to minimize these, since they are a major contributor to the pollutants left after burning. Pretreatment of the waste by physical or chemical means may be necessary.

3) What is the heating value of the waste? Since the temperature of the burn is critical in limiting polluting air emissions, it must be determined that the mixture of wastes and, if necessary, special fuels used in the unit will maintain a high enough temperature. Rich organic liquids and organic sludges (with solid content 20 percent or more by weight) have heating values high enough to maintain combustion without adding fuel. Lean organic liquids do not have enough heating value to maintain combustion; other materials must be added to the thermal destruction unit for complete combustion. Often a proper mixing of waste streams can take care of the heat value problem without adding expensive special fuels. For example, solvent wastes, which have a high heating value, can be burnt with low heating value wastes such as aqueous solutions containing hazardous organics. The cost of burning the waste usually increases as the heating value of the waste decreases.

Many kinds of thermal destruction units are in use today or under experimentation. Some of these technologies are capable of handling a wide variety of wastes; others have very specific uses. If properly operated and designed, and if the correct pollution control equipment is installed, thermal destruction can be an essential part of the waste management system. It cannot, however, be the final part of the waste management system; the process leaves behind residues that need additional disposal precautions to protect the environment.

III: Solidification/Encapsulation

Traditionally, residues left over from the previously described processes have simply been dumped into landfills. Fortunately, methods that lessen the likelihood of residues escaping into the environment after they have been landfilled have been developed. These methods, called solidification or encapsulation, bind the waste residues into solid form by mixing or coating them with other materials before placing them in the landfill. Inorganic materials high in heavy metals and salts are suited for treatment by this method. The ash by-products of incineration usually fit this description. Wastes that contain greater than 10 to 20 percent organic materials are not good candidates for stabilization processes.

Much concern has been expressed about whether the wastes will remain solidified in the long term. There are fears that weathering, physical and biological factors, and other wastes in the surrounding soil will eventually break down the solidified materials. Because of these uncertainties, solidified and encapsulated materials need to be carefully monitored. Another unfortunate consequence of solidification is an increase in the volume of material left over to be stored. Nevertheless, hazardous waste residues should never be disposed of in landfills without being subjected first to solidification or encapsulation processes.

IV: Landfilling

Past and present experience has shown that wastes inevitably leak from landfills. The U.S. Environmental Protection Agency asserts:

> ... the regulation of hazardous waste land disposal must proceed from the assumption that migration of hazardous wastes and their constituents and by-products from a land disposal facility will inevitably occur.[18]

Unfortunately, landfilling has been the most widely used disposal option.

Nevertheless, some industrial wastes will have to be landfilled. The potential problems of landfilling can be minimized by adherence to the three following principles.

Liquid wastes should not be put into a landfill. When in a liquid state, wastes can easily move from their initial location, permanently contaminating nearby ground and surface water. Technologies are available to solidify liquids before disposal.

The second principle of landfill operation is that hazardous wastes should not enter a landfill unless they have been fully

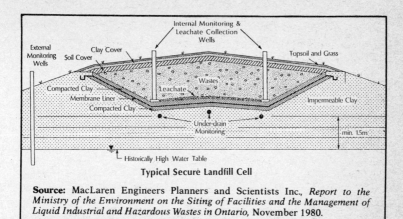

Typical Secure Landfill Cell

Source: MacLaren Engineers Planners and Scientists Inc., *Report to the Ministry of the Environment on the Siting of Facilities and the Management of Liquid Industrial and Hazardous Wastes in Ontario,* November 1980.

treated to reduce their volume and toxicity. Only after employing all possible recycling and reuse technologies and all potential treatment methods, should the remaining treated waste be considered for landfilling.

The third principle of landfill operation is that no highly hazardous materials should be disposed of in this manner. Even after the use of all available treatment technologies, some wastes remain so hazardous to the environment that no risk of their leaking from a landfill can be afforded.

From the many examples presented so far, it should be clear that there are many problems associated with the sites used for landfilling. A site may be poorly chosen or designed; its improper operation may include the mixing of incompatible wastes or inadequate monitoring; and such problems might be further compounded by the collection of leachate. Soil conditions, topography, hydrogeologic conditions, geologic conditions, and climatic conditions all influence the ability of a landfill to isolate wastes from the environment.

The major problem posed by improper landfill is the production of contaminant-bearing liquids, called leachate. Leachate often moves from a landfill into the surrounding soil and water. Production of these liquids can be reduced by sloping the surface of the landfill to reduce the probability of surface runoff from precipitation soaking into the landfill, and by burying only non-soluble hazardous wastes. The leachate problem can also be reduced by locating landfills where the groundwater level is at great depths, or where there is a thick layer of impervious soil, such as clay, which will prevent or slow down the movement of leachate. An artificial barrier around the landfill may contain the leachate. A leachate-collection system can be used to catch the liquid at the bottom and sides of the landfill and to pump it to the surface for retreatment.

Properly operated landfills have two other important features: a monitoring system and a contingency plan. The monitoring includes thorough testing of wastes to make sure they are suitable for landfilling. Constant monitoring of nearby ground water is also essential in order to provide an early warning of contamination and to allow for action. The contingency plan outlines in detail the measures to be taken if contamination of the environment occurs.

The possibilities for taking corrective action are increased if waste types are buried in separate cells in the landfill and records are kept of where the wastes have been buried. If the leachate shows a particular waste is creating problems, it may be possible to remove it. Separation of wastes also minimizes leachate production since the contact of wastes with each other may cause reactions that counteract the stabilizing treatments that they have previously undergone. In addition, it may be desirable to dig up the wastes if new processes for treatment or reuse are developed.

Substitution

INDUSTRY HAS OFTEN REGARDED landfilling as the only option for hazardous waste disposal. Apart from the fact that this ignores other proven methods, experience has indicated that landfilling presents considerable dangers.

Frequently, even those sincerely concerned about the protection of the environment call landfilling "the measure of last resort," but some materials, even after all available treatment, remain too hazardous to be deposited in landfills. When this is the case, two questions need to be asked: 1) can a different production process be used that will avoid the production of that particular hazardous waste? and 2) if there is no alternative safe method of production, is the need for the item being produced worth the environmental and health risks?

Materials used in some production processes have been changed because of the hazards they produce. In the paint industry, solvents have been widely used for many years. Serious concerns have been raised about the health effects of these solvents on workers in the plant and on the people who live in the community where paint wastes are disposed. Some manufacturers have developed paints with all or part of the solvent base absent. A Vancouver company, Flecto Coatings Ltd., has reduced the solvent component of its paint to about 20 percent by weight; the solvent component of paints has commonly been 60 to 80 percent.[19] In many production processes, relatively harmless materials can be substituted for more hazardous ones.

Substitution of one material for another may not always be possible. It must then be decided whether the risks associated with production should be taken. The Canadian federal government under the *Environment Contaminants Act* has the power to ban or restrict the production or use of a substance that is proven to be "a significant danger to human health and the environment". In three instances — Mirex, PBBs and PCTs — the Canadian government has used this power to ban the production and use of hazardous materials.

Instituting a New Waste Management System

IF THE SIX STEPS OUTLINED ABOVE were carefully followed, the tragedy that hazardous waste disposal has become would be significantly reduced. The methods described in this chapter are not new. Two factors, however, have impeded their being used to their full potential. Governments are reluctant to intrude into corporate decision-making, and as a result, government regulations and guidelines have been too weak. Without strict government controls, industry will not place a strong emphasis on environmental protection.

The second factor that works against this system is cost. For most companies, landfilling is the cheapest means of waste disposal. A 1976 U.S. Federal government survey of six types of industries reported "92 percent of the wastes were deposited on land at an average cost of $11 per ton, 4 percent were recycled at $19 per ton, and 4 percent were treated at $49 per ton."[20] Landfill is cheap only because all the costs involved in using this method are not charged to the company. The long term societal costs of contamination and the expensive procedures needed for long-term care of wastes are not included. A senior administrator with the U.S. Environmental Protection Agency described the situation:

> Government policy and industrial practices generally favored environmentally unsound disposal of wastes, hazardous or not, because the cost of environmental and health damage did not appear in the expense ledgers of business and government.[21]

Cost is the deciding factor in corporate waste disposal decisions; when the costs created by unsafe practices are not added to the original disposal costs, negligent behaviour is encouraged.

A new waste management system will be implemented only when government regulations urge it to happen and when disposal costs accurately reflect the impacts of improper hazardous waste handling.

Industry says waste is an inevitable by-product of production. Proper production planning, therefore, includes plans for handling wastes. It is at the pre-production stage that options can be fully considered, most effectively put into operation, and most cheaply instituted.

CHAPTER SEVEN
CONCLUSION

DEVASTATION OF OUR ENVIRONMENT confronts us daily. PCBs have become a normal part of the air we breathe. Lakes die as a result of acid rain. Chemical contaminants permeate the Great Lakes. Serious questions are raised about the quality of the water we drink, even by those whose citified water supply is supposedly purified. Cancer is reaching near epidemic proportions. One after another, species of wild life become extinct as their habitats are destroyed by the intrusion of so-called civilization. The land turns to lifeless concrete as it is pounded by the giant farming factories.

But a new awareness is arising. Daily, more and more people are realizing that we are an integral part of nature, that nature's well-being is also our well-being. As a result, demands are being made that the careless practices of the past be stopped and that the environment be treated with care.

Unfortunately, this changing consciousness does not always correspond with changed priorities in decision-making. The effects of a leaking toxic waste dump are of greater concern to people who live next door to it than to those who own and manage the factories producing the wastes. Similarly, workers whose health may be affected by chemicals in a plant are more anxious to remove the contaminants than are the owners who have to pay for protective measures. Invariably those who make the final decisions — the people who sit in corporate board rooms and in government cabinet meetings — put a lesser weight upon the importance of pollution prevention than do those who are most directly affected by the pollution.

Nevertheless, pollution practices are gradually changing. There are fewer companies trying to dump untreated hazardous wastes into nearby streams. Many companies are now recycling rather than simply dumping all wastes into landfills. But this behaviour is not necessarily the result of the companies themselves placing a higher priority upon pollution prevention. They act this way when forced by government regulations and when government and public surveillance make them realize they are likely to be caught and penalized if they do not abide by such regulations. They also act this way when shown that pollution prevention can be profitable. The rising costs of disposal, the removal of the cheapest of these options — pouring them into streams and onto the ground — and the increased costs of material inputs encourage companies to make decisions that reduce the amounts of wastes produced. Potentially these factors will have important impacts upon the hazardous wastes problem. These decisions, however, are still based on the ability to make profits.

The changing consciousness among the general public is a promising sign. This consciousness, however, will not translate into an improved quality of life until decision-making is affected. As a result of persistent public demand, formal public hearings are becoming a widely accepted practice. In addition to this right to be heard, citizens have been pushing for their right to information. Most government jurisdictions already consider access to basic government information a legitimate right, but now the public is pressing for right of access to private corporation information as well. The demand for "right to know" legislation, which grants the public the right to know all information about toxic substances held by companies, is a rising movement in the U.S. and is being seriously considered in some parts of Canada.

These two rights — the right to know and the right to be heard — are gradually being introduced. However, if they are to be more than mere window dressing, they must be considerably strengthened. The effectiveness of the citizens' right to be heard at public meetings will not be fully realized unless they are provided with the financial means for well-researched or expert input.

The right to participate in decisions is not granted the public until the wastes have already been produced. As a result, citizens are confronted with a problem for which the best and often the only effective solution — reducing the quantities produced — has already been missed. The situation with most contaminants is similar. Citizens must have the opportunity to become involved in the pre-production stage of decision making.

Corporations should be required to present pre-production plans to the government. In these plans, the company should be forced to take into account the potential impacts of its actions upon all sectors of society and the environment. These plans should include waste disposal programmes, worker protection plans and effluent control measures. All these plans should be public. Everyone should have the opportunity to review and provide feedback on these plans. The government should then insist on changes in the company's production proposals in order to protect the public and the environment. These agreements should be made known to the public. The right to participate in basic corporate decisions is the only way the public can truly protect itself from the ravages of industry.

Agreements that are not stringently enforced are useless. Experience shows that such enforcement cannot be taken for granted. People in the community should have a role to play in the enforcement process. For example, some of the people who opposed the dump in Glanbrook, Ontario, sit on the Township's landfill monitoring committee. Similarly, in the Niagara area, citizens from both the U.S. and Canada have become part of an official committee that will monitor the discharges of SCA's waste treatment plant into the Niagara River. The company has been forced to cover the costs of the citizens' testing programme.

Unfortunately, these changes do not of themselves guarantee that decision-making will improve. Many times citizens have gone to public hearings, made substantial input and left feeling confident that their arguments were so convincing that a good decision would inevitably be made. Months later, when the decision is finally announced, they are left wondering if the government was ever in the same room as they were. The benefit of the doubt is too often given to the company. Clearly, the sympathies of the government decision-makers are with the corporations, not with the public. When the decision is heard, the reality of where power truly lies comes thundering home.

Those who have directly participated in the decision-making process through the forums set up to allow public input leave the experience disillusioned. In some instances people were actually able to stop a dangerous and irresponsible plan, but even this does not restore the public's faith in the decision-making process. The people of South Cayuga were able to get the government to withdraw its plans to build a liquid waste disposal facility beside the flood-prone Grand River. After the favourable decision, one resident who went through that year-long process said:

> I feel the government has to be pulled into responsibility. The government would have been irresponsible if there hadn't been resistance.[1]

Increasingly people throughout North America are offering resistance. Not only is this occurring among those who live near toxic waste dumps but also among people living next to an area being sprayed by pesticides, by workers in a factory where chemicals are used, and in numerous other places. They begin by asking questions and making suggestions to government through normally defined routes. But frustration soon builds. The transition of feelings experienced by Lillian Tomen of Harwich Township corresponds with that of innumerable other people:

> In the beginning we thought that our government could do no wrong. We figured what the government says is always right because they were elected by the people and we felt they were serving the people's requests and the people's needs. But when we started digging into it and found out what they had allowed to happen, then we were disillusioned. We felt we couldn't trust them anymore.[2]

As this disillusionment deepens, the people develop a true campaign. Massive education is undertaken to make everyone in the community aware of what is going on and of the potential impacts. Demonstrations are held to place pressure on the decision-makers. One rainy April morning, 1,000 people turned out at a rally in Whitchurch-Stouffville to make the government aware of their concerns about the extension of a company's licence to operate a dump. In Harwich Township, 1,000 farmers came out on a bright August morning to voice their anger with a proposal for a solidification plant.

As the frustration builds, tactics sometimes shift from lobbying to active resistance. When the government blatantly ignored a court ruling that the Harwich landfill was operating illegally, the people stopped the Browning-Ferris operation by blocking the dump entrance with tractors. A second court hearing finally brought about a ban on dumping liquid wastes at the landfill. Actions of this nature are likely to increase in frequency as people become more aware of the need to assert their decision-making power.

Already we can see shifts in that power. Concessions, though they may be minor, are being made. Responsibilities that never before were accepted by corporations are now being required of them by government because it is being forced to place more weight on the citizens' perspective than it did in the past. But there is still a long way to go.

Frequently government plays one group against another by saying that someone must assume the risks of hazardous wastes. This tactic shifts power back to corporate boardrooms. Concerned citizens are getting around this problem by working together. In Ontario, thirteen groups from across southern Ontario have been meeting on a regular basis during 1982. They have gotten to know each other, to understand the specific problems of the others, and to recognize that their problem is not an isolated one but part of a pattern. The recognition that they are all victims of a common decision-making pattern has made them realize that just fighting to protect their own community is not the solution. It is by working together to change the basis upon which decisions are made that they will solve the problem. They have now begun to support each other in their specific fights. For example, the Whitchurch-Stouffville demonstration was attended by people from over 200 miles away. In addition, they are appearing as a united front before the Ontario Ministry of the Environment and the Ontario Waste Management Corporation to make specific recommendations. In their August 1982 meeting with the Minister of the Environment, Keith Norton, they stressed the need to take actions that will help all people in Ontario, not just the people of Hamilton or Niagara or Sarnia or Whitchurch-Stouffville or Harwich. This working together will inevitably strengthen their influence in decision-making.

People are also realizing that the decision-making biases that create their problems are similar from problem to problem. For example, it is the same corporations and the same governments that place less value on the health of workers and on residents next to a hazardous waste dump than they do on profits that can be made by minimizing expenditures on engineering equipment designed to reduce pollution in both the workplace and the community. Likewise those concerned about different environmental issues discover that they are all fighting the same limited outlooks and biased decision-making structures. As this recognition deepens and spreads, those involved come more clearly to recognize that what they are really after is a change in decision-making. Divergent groups can start working together to support each other in their specific struggles and to force government to act in a responsible manner.

The hazardous waste problem and other environmental problems in our society can be eliminated. But this change will only happen when the burden of proof shifts from the public to the corporations creating the problems. So often citizens say, "We have to prove what we say; government believes industry." This situation must be reversed.

As members of this society, citizens have the right to make decisions which affect their lives. In those places where people are organizing and working together this right is being made a reality.

APPENDIX
HAZARDOUS WASTES ACROSS CANADA

THROUGHOUT CANADA, HAZARDOUS WASTES are produced and improperly discarded. Instances of illegal dumping abound; likewise contamination of water supplies can be found all across the country. In this appendix, the quantities and types of wastes produced are described; disposal sites and government plans for changes in handling of wastes, if any, are also presented. Unfortunately, the available information is far from complete. No one knows what is happening to all the wastes in this country.

In January 1982, the Canadian federal government released a study that a consulting firm, Gore & Storrie, had conducted for Environment Canada.[1] By making estimates based on the types and sizes of industries in each part of Canada, this report stated the quantities of hazardous wastes that are probably produced. The descriptions of quantities and types of wastes in this appendix are derived from the Gore & Storrie report. The quantities are measured in wet tonnes; one wet tonne is approximately 220 Imperial gallons.

The Gore & Storrie report said nothing about how wastes are handled. Undoubtedly, the overwhelming majority are put into landfill sites — most of which have not been specially designed to handle such wastes. Many wastes are disposed of at the plant where they are produced without being taken to an outside landfill or other disposal facility. Disposal on the company's property does not, however, mean that the effects of that disposal are confined to the company's private property. Air and water contamination frequently moves from the site to surrounding neighbourhoods.

Government regulation of hazardous waste disposal varies from province to province. Most provinces do not have special regulations for handling and disposal of hazardous wastes. They are simply treated in the same way as residential garbage. Licensing procedures for disposal sites vary. Several provinces do not require public hearings before sites can be operated. In some instances, public hearings are required if the facility is to be operated by a government body (provincial or municipal), but not in the case of a proposal by a private company. Only Ontario has a waybill system, which attempts to keep track of where hazardous wastes are disposed.

NEWFOUNDLAND

Since its economy is based on fishing, Newfoundland is not a major generator of hazardous wastes. It is estimated that 20,719 tonnes of hazardous wastes are produced here yearly. Ninety-five percent of this waste is from phosphorus manufacturing at Long Harbour. Other industries that contribute to this total include wood preserving, blast furnaces, and the manufacture of polyethylene pots.

THE MARITIMES

In 1980, the federal government's Environmental Protection Service estimated that 65 percent of hazardous wastes in the three maritime provinces of Prince Edward Island, Nova Scotia, and New Brunswick were disposed of by unacceptable methods.[2] One-half of the wastes were dumped untreated into municipal landfills and dumps. The Environmental Protection Service surveyed some companies' disposal practices. Of the 153 surveyed companies disposing wastes into municipal landfills and dumps, 130 or 85 percent were unacceptable. Some companies put their wastes into sewers; all seven such cases examined were discharging unacceptable effluent into the sewage system.

The head of Environment Canada's Atlantic Region office remarked that "the present lack of facilities and controls in this area [the maritimes] make daylight dumping much easier."[3] The federal government suggested that central treatment and disposal facilities be developed to handle hazardous wastes from throughout the three maritime provinces. The suggestion was that they be located in Cumberland County in Nova Scotia. The province of Nova Scotia, however, has not supported this suggestion. A 1982 Nova Scotia Department of Environment report concluded that "the economic, financial and social feasibility of a central, maritime hazardous waste disposal facility is not demonstrated by the Inventory [the federal government's *Maritime Hazardous Waste Inventory Report*]."[4]

In addition to suggesting the development of a central disposal facility, the federal government urged the maritime provinces to promote both resource recovery and waste exchange programmes.

It estimated that one-quarter of the wastes presently being unsafely disposed of could be handled by these methods.[5]

PRINCE EDWARD ISLAND

Approximately 406 tonnes of hazardous wastes are produced annually in Prince Edward Island. Almost half these wastes come from the CIL fertilizer plant at O'Leary Station. Two other major contributors are a chemicals plant and a stainless steel cookware producer in Charlottetown.

NOVA SCOTIA

Almost half of Nova Scotia's 106,857 tonnes of annual waste production comes from the three heavy water plants in the province. Another 30 percent is the result of production at the Sydney Steel Plant. The sources of some of the province's most hazardous substances including paint sludge, latex, PCBs and pesticides are concentrated in the Halifax area.

At present the majority of these wastes are dumped into landfills. At one such dumpsite near Amherst, PCBs are leaking into a nearby river.[6]

NEW BRUNSWICK

Each year, 46,885 tonnes of hazardous wastes are produced in New Brunswick. Just over 40 percent of these wastes is generated by the Irving oil refinery at St. John. One-third of the wastes comes from the six pulp and paper mills in the province. Chemical wastes from potash, aluminum, plastics, and chemical production also create a significant proportion of the province's hazardous wastes stream.

New Brunswick's Environment Department concluded in 1982 that less than 20 percent of the province's hazardous wastes was disposed of in an environmentally sound manner.[7] Despite the report's urging of additional staff to allow for stricter policing of hazardous waste disposal, the province's environment minister said, "It is not in the budget estimates of my department. In fact, we just completed a manpower review trying to cut down."[8]

QUEBEC

Almost one million tonnes of hazardous wastes are produced yearly in Quebec. Over half of this material is chemical waste from a variety of operations including solvent production, insecticides companies, chemical producers and explosives manufacturers. Almost two-thirds of these chemical wastes are produced in the Montreal area. Metal wastes from various metal fabrication operations and the production of aluminum also are major contributors to Quebec's hazardous wastes.

Many instances of illegal dumping of hazardous wastes have been reported in Quebec. Because of a lack of suitable treatment facilities, the Quebec government in 1978 asked approximately 5,000 companies to store their chemical wastes at their plants while the government sought methods to safely dispose of them.[9] In addition, twenty companies have been licensed to gather these wastes and store them. Storage is in tanks, at transfer stations and in supposedly temporary open pits. A physical/chemical treatment and solidification plant for inorganic wastes and a landfill are being built by Stablex Canada Ltd. at Blainville, 15 miles north of Montreal. It is scheduled to begin receiving wastes in the Fall of 1983. An incinerator is operated by Tricil near Mercier, southwest of Montreal, to burn organic wastes. Testing in 1982 indicated serious problems with emissions from this facility.[10] In September 1982, the provincial government issued a call for proposals from private companies to set up incineration or recycling facilities for organic wastes.

ONTARIO

One half of the hazardous wastes produced in Canada come from Ontario — 1,605,107 tonnes annually. Fifty percent of these wastes are generated in the Toronto and Hamilton areas.[11]

In 1982, eight landfills in the province had licences to receive liquid industrial wastes. A Tricil incinerator near Sarnia also was licensed to accept hazardous wastes. The province has set up a crown corporation that has the responsibility to develop and manage waste disposal facilities. That corporation expects to have specific proposals for facilities by the summer of 1983.

WESTERN AND NORTHERN CANADA

A 1980 study conducted for Environment Canada by the Reid, Crowther consulting company recommended that an integrated disposal system be set up for hazardous wastes throughout the provinces and northern Ontario.[12] The proposal suggested that one incinerator with secure landfill be located near the Alberta-Saskatchewan border to serve the entire region. In addition, it was recommended that a physical-treatment plant be set up in each of the four provinces. These physical-treatment plants would be located near a major area of waste generation in each province.

This integrated plan for the western provinces has not been acted upon. Instead both Alberta and British Columbia are trying to develop major facilities to handle their own wastes without taking into account the possibility of shipping wastes to or receiving them from other provinces.

MANITOBA

Twenty-nine thousand tonnes of hazardous wastes are produced annually in Manitoba. One-third of these wastes comes from the two oil refineries in Winnipeg. Tanneries, plastics manufacturers, and the pulp and paper industry also make substantial contributions to this total. Almost two-thirds of Manitoba's hazardous wastes are generated in Winnipeg.

Rural municipalities around Winnipeg report that "commercial operators and individuals are dumping waste materials illegally in rural areas."[13] Manitoba's hazardous wastes are being handled in three ways: 1) landfill, 2) transportation out of the province, and 3) storage in an old aircraft fuel tank in the small town of Gimli located on the shore of Lake Winnipeg about 50 miles north of Winnipeg.[14]

SASKATCHEWAN

The primarily wheat farming province of Saskatchewan produces 30,144 tonnes of hazardous wastes each year. Almost half of these wastes are produced by a steel pipe manufacturer in Regina. Oil refining, chemical production, and fertilizer production are also major sources of wastes.

There are approximately 650 dump sites in the province.[15] Many of these are creating problems. For example, there is concern that ground water below Saskatoon is contaminated with chemical wastes leaching from deep-wells that were used for disposal between 1963 and 1977.[16] Most wastes go into landfills.

ALBERTA

Alberta annually produces 215,944 tonnes of hazardous wastes. Sixty percent is chemical wastes; the manufacture of fertilizers, methanol, ethylene, and acetates are the principal sources of these wastes. Gas and oil refineries make up about 10 percent of the provincial waste totals. Over 3000 tonnes of herbicide wastes are produced annually in Alberta. One-third of the province's hazardous wastes comes from Edmonton.

Most hazardous wastes in Alberta are deposited into landfills. The Environmental Council of Alberta concluded in 1980 that "disposal of solid and liquid wastes on land is largely uncontrolled by legislation. Large volumes of the solids, sludges and liquids are put directly into landfills which are not suitable for them."[17] The bulk of these hazardous wastes is sent to the Clover Bar and Forest Lawn landfills in Edmonton and Calgary respectively. An Environment Alberta spokesperson said in 1980, "There are no protective measures to isolate the landfill operation [at Forest Lawn] from the environment beneath."[18] Many smaller landfill sites, particularly in rural areas, are known to receive hazardous wastes. Some refinery and petrochemical wastes are injected into deep wells. A small incinerator at the University of Alberta in Edmonton has a burning capacity of fifty gallons an hour. There is a PCB storage site at Nisku and some problem wastes are shipped to the United States.

The Alberta government plans to develop one major waste treatment complex for the whole province. This facility will include incineration, solidification, and landfilling. Throughout 1982, the province undertook a programme to try to establish public support for the location of such facilities. It has received a mixed response.

BRITISH COLUMBIA

It is estimated that British Columbia's annual production of wastes is 273,425 tonnes. Over half these wastes are metal — the highest proportion in Canada. The aluminum smelter at Kitimat alone generates one-quarter of these wastes. Two metal smelters and refineries at Richmond are also major contributors.

In 1981, a B.C. government report stated that the lower Fraser River is "a filthy mess of illegal dumping and toxic wastes piling up for 25 years."[19] Although most hazardous wastes are put into landfills, an Environment Canada report concluded that "B.C. does not have a secure landfill capable of accepting hazardous wastes."[20] Some pesticide wastes and PCBs are gathered at Kamloops by the provincial government and shipped to a landfill in Oregon. It is estimated that this amounts to about 300 barrels each year. In 1978, a recycling company went bankrupt and left an estimated 100,000 to 150,000 gallons of hazardous wastes in barrels leaking and rotting in two fields in a Vancouver suburb.[21]

The provincial government is encouraging private companies to develop a major waste disposal facility. In early 1982, it wrote to 22 companies asking them to submit proposals for such facilities.

YUKON TERRITORY

The only known source of hazardous wastes in the Yukon is an oxygen and acetylene company in Whitehorse. It produces approximately 1,000 tonnes of chemical wastes each year.

GLOSSARY

bioaccumulation — the increased concentration and accumulation of chemical substances in organisms.

drumlin — a hill of glacial drift or bedrock formed into a streamlined shape much like an upturned spoon. This geological formation allows easier access of liquids into groundwater aquifers below.

inorganic — a substance in which the chemical building block, carbon, is not present (for example, sulphur dioxide: SO_2).

International Joint Commission (IJC) — a binational organization established in 1909 by the Boundary Waters Treaty between Canada and the United States. The commission was created to deal with boundary water problems including those of the Great Lakes and consists of three Canadian and three U.S. commissioners.

lagoon — a shallow pond. In most cases in this book, it refers to an artifical pool for containing liquid wastes.

leachate — the mineral- or metal-laden liquid created when groundwater moves through a waste site dissolving soluble materials.

Mirex — the generic name for a pesticide used on fire ants which now has only restricted use because of its highly toxic nature.

organic — a substance containing carbon compounds. The carbon is usually connected to hydrogen atoms (for example, toluene: $C_6H_5CH_3$).

phenol — a highly poisonous class of organic chemicals that have a distinctive odor and sharp burning taste. They are used to make resins, weed killers and as a solvent and chemical intermediary.

pickle liquor — a solution, usually consisting of sulphuric or hydrochloric acid, which various metals are dipped into to remove scale, or other impurities from the surface. The highly acidic nature of this material necessitates that it be handled carefully.

PBBs — Polybrominated Biphenyls were formerly used as a flame retardent and in polyester resins, polystyrene, polyethelene and polyester fibres. It has been shown to seriously affect the reproduction of birds and mammals, and in 1973, after accidentally being mixed into animal feed, caused the death and sickness of a large number of livestock in Michigan. PBBs have subsequently been highly restricted in use by Environment Canada.

PCBs — Polychlorinated Biphenyls are a highly toxic, colourless liquid used as an insulating fluid in electrical equipment.

PCTs — Polychlorinated Terphenyls were used commercially as a component of pressure sensitive backing for weather stripping and as a plasticizer for urethane and paints. It has been shown to accumulate in the liver and other tissues of test animals and consequently Environment Canada has restricted all commercial, manufacturing, and processing uses.

toxic metals — particular metals which have serious harmful effects on the human body. Some of the most toxic metals are: cadmium, mercury, lead, barium, chromium, and beryllium.

References

Introduction
[1] Quoted in "Farmer still bitter over cattle deaths," *Kitchener-Waterloo Record,* 9 August 1980, p. 35. Information concerning this example was compiled by Cyndie Obie.
[2] Stan Irwin, quoted by Ron McCurdy and Ron Eade, "Cleanup breathes life into Elmira creek," *Kitchener-Waterloo Record,* 9 August 1980, p. 35.
[3] William Marsden, "Waste dump threatens towns, rich farmland," *Montreal Gazette,* 27 March 1982, p. B2.
[4] George Buitenwerf, quoted by Bill Johnston, "I saw PCBs, cyanide go to Ottawa dump," *Spectator* [Hamilton], 6 October 1980.
[5] Frank Jones, "Toxic horrors in Hamilton's backyard," *Toronto Star,* 5 October 1980, p. A10, and Gord McNulty, "MLAs burned at radioactive waste disposal," *Spectator,* 25 July 1979, p. 7.
[6] Based on telephone interview with Jim Dochstader, industrial abatement officer, Sarnia office, Ministry of the Environment, April 1982.
[7] Jim Dochstader, quoted by Doug Firby and Brian Fox, "Danger lurks under Sarnia subdivision," *Windsor Star,* 11 July 1981, p. B12.
[8] Quoted by Victoria Cross Hughley, "Your health or your job," *Detroit Metro Times,* 4 February 1982, p. 5.
[9] "The Poisoning of Canada," *Canadian Dimension,* May 1982, p. 3.
[10] Authors' interview, July 1982.

Chapter 1: The Hazardous Wastes Problem
[1] Michael Keating, "800 'lost' dumps are tracked down; contents unknown," *Globe and Mail,* 11 December 1979.
[2] Fred C. Hart Associates, Inc., *Preliminary Assessment of Cleanup Costs for National Hazardous Waste Problems,* 1979, p. 25.
[3] Managing Chemical Waste: What we're doing about it, [undated], p. 7.
[4] "The Toxic Tragedy," in *Who's Poisoning America,* ed. Ralph Nader *et al* (San Francisco: Sierra Club Books, 1981), p. 24.
[5] Gore & Storrie Limited, *Canadian National Inventory of Hazardous and Toxic Wastes* (Ottawa: Environment Canada, 1982), vol. 3, p. 8.
[6] General Accounting Office, *EPA is Slow to Carry Out Its Responsibility to Control Hazardous Chemicals,* 28 October 1980, p. 20.
[7] New York Academy of Sciences, *Cancer and the Worker* (New York, 1977), p. 69.

[8] *The Politics of Cancer,* rev. ed. (New York: Anchor Press/Doubleday, 1979), p. 27.

[9] Transport Canada, Transport Dangerous Goods Branch, *Summary of 1980 and 1981 Accidents on File.*

[10] *Ibid.*

[11] Environment Council of Alberta, *Hazardous Waste Management in Alberta,* December 1980, p. 70.

[12] *Ecotoxicity: Responsibilities and Opportunities,* August 1979, p. 2.

[13] *Great Lakes Water Quality Report, Appendix E, Status Report on Organic and Heavy Metal Contaminants in Lakes Erie, Michigan, Huron, and Superior Basin,* July 1978.

[14] Quoted in "Great Lakes cleaner but chemicals multiply," *Globe and Mail,* 11 October 1980, p. 4.

[15] Peter Rickwood, "Deadly dioxin found in human a first in North America," *Toronto Star,* 24 June 1982.

[16] CTV, "The Failing Strategy," 11 December 1977.

[17] *Ecotoxicity, op. cit.,* p. 3.

[18] *Alternatives to the Land Disposal of Hazardous Wastes: An Assessment for California,* 1981, p. 57.

[19] Ontario Waste Management Corporation, *Waste Quantities Study,* August 1982, p. 32.

[20] Statement by Boris Boyko in interview, November 1981.

[21] *Ibid.*

[22] Gore & Storrie Limited, *op. cit.,* vol. 3, p. 8.

[23] Figures in this paragraph are derived from Ontario Waste Management Corporation, *op. cit.,* p. 32.

[24] *Facilities Development Process: Phase 1 Report,* September 1982, Figure 5 opposite p. 17.

[25] *Ibid.*

[26] Telephone interview with Harry Sharp of D&D Disposal, October 1982.

[27] Telephone interview with Debra Irwin, Information Officer, Ontario Hydro, October 1982.

[28] Art Kilgour, "Uranium Mining: Who Pays, Who Profits?", *The Birch Bark Alliance* 4, pp. 6-8.

[29] Daniel Stoffman, "Deadly nuclear waste piles up," *Toronto Star,* 7 November 1982.

[30] Paul Mckay, "Nuclear dumps leak into Lake Ontario," *Birch Bark Alliance* 8, p. 1.

[31] Patricia Lawson, "Mismanagement of Radioactive Wastes," Science and the Environment Conference, November 1977.

[32] Penny Sanger, *Blind Faith,* (Toronto: McGraw-Hill Ryerson, 1981), p. 164.

[33] Art Kilgour, "The Scarborough Story: A-dirt without a home," *Birch Bark Alliance,* Fall 1981, p. 7.

[34] Quoted in *ibid.*

[35] Telephone interview with Mr. Geeky, Canadian Medical Association.

[36] Jane O'Hara, "Don't Drink the Water," *Maclean's,* 22 June 1981, p. 26.

[37] "Health Hazards at Love Canal," Testimony presented to the House Sub-Committee on Oversight and Investigations, 21 March 1979.

[38] *Ibid.*, p. 21.
[39] Josh Barbanel, "At Love Canal, despair is the pervasive affliction," *New York Times,* 19 May 1980.
[40] *Laying Waste: The Poisoning of America by Toxic Chemicals,* (New York: Washington Square Press, 1981), p. 65.
[41] Quoted by Betty Burcher, "No Love Canals Here," *Healthsharing,* Winter 1980, p. 10.
[42] Hedy Gervais, quoted in *ibid.,* p. 8.
[43] *Ibid.,* and "I saw PCBs, cyanide go to Ottawa dump," *Spectator* [Hamilton], 6 October 1980.
[44] Kevin Marron, "Dump is poison, woman in Hamilton warns," *Globe and Mail,* 21 December 1979, p. 9.

Chapter 2: The Waste Management Industry

[1] Don Fitch, quoted by Mark Schleifstein and Cliff Treyens, "Empire of Waste," *Clarion-Ledger* [Jackson, Mississippi], 3 December 1980, p. 29.
[2] *Ibid.,* p. 32.
[3] *Moody's Handbook of Common Stocks* (New York: Moody's Investors Services, Inc., Spring 1982).
[4] Hon. S.H.S. Hughes, *Report of the Royal Commission Appointed to Inquire into Waste Management Inc., et cetera,* 30 March 1978, pp. 17-18.
[5] *Moody's Handbook of Common Stocks, op. cit.*
[6] U.S. Congress, House, *Hearing before the Subcommittee on Oversight and Investigations of the Committee on Energy and Commerce,* testimony of John M. Fox, Chairman, SCA Services, Inc., 28 May 1981, pp. 56-60.
[7] *50,000 Leading U.S. Corporations* (Baldwin H. Ward Publications, 1980).
[8] "Laidlaw to consolidate waste management in U.S. unit," *Globe and Mail,* 21 January 1982, p. B8.
[9] *Ibid.*
[10] 5 May 1980.
[11] *Ibid.*
[12] *Moody's Handbook of Common Stocks, op.cit.*
[13] *Clarion-Ledger,* 3 December 1980, p. 26.
[14] "A legal time bomb for corporations," *Business Week,* 16 June 1980, p. 150.
[15] Telephone interview, May 1982.
[16] *Ibid.*
[17] Interview with Jim Stewart, Chemical and Petro Waste Disposal Ltd., Barrie, January 1982.
[18] *Managing Chemical Wastes,* p. 8.
[19] Mark Schleifstein and Cliff Treyens, *op.cit.*
[20] *Ibid.,* p. 32.
[21] "Company to appeal landfill site closure; cites water quality," *Globe and Mail,* 14 May 1982.
[22] Authors' interview, December 1981.
[23] "Charges allege toxic dumping," *Globe and Mail,* 2 October 1982.
[24] "Trim toxic waste, Tricil is ordered," *Gazette* [Montreal], 12 October 1982.
[25] *Managing Chemical Waste,* p. 6.
[26] Authors' interview with Jim Stewart, January 1982.

Chapter 3: Government Control of Hazardous Wastes

[1] Gwen Smith, "Unlicenced waste tank on farm keeps filling up," *Globe and Mail*, 6 September 1980.
[2] Documents released by the Township, March 1981.
[3] *Ibid.*
[4] Quoted in a letter from Harwich Township Clerk-Treasurer to Minister of the Environment, 23 September 1980.
[5] Telephone interview with Jim Dochstader, April 1982.
[6] Authors' interview with Jim Stewart, January 1982.
[7] Quoted by Gwen Smith, "Ontario's controls on waste called 'a game of sham'," *Globe and Mail*, 26 August 1980, p. 5.
[8] Ed Turner, quoted by John Lymburner, "Phantom Dumpers," *Civic*, December 1977, p. 26.
[9] "Ministry admitted industrial waste at site: Official," *Toronto Star*, 2 June 1982.
[10] *Ibid.*
[11] Gore & Storrie Limited, *Canadian National Inventory of Hazardous and Toxic Wastes*, vol. 3, p. 53.
[12] "Waste volumes to be studied," *Toronto Star*, 23 December 1981.
[13] Ontario Waste Management Corporation, *Waste Quantities Study*, August 1982.
[14] *Environmental Assessment for Solidification Facilities in Harwich Township and in the City of Niagara Falls*, 1980, vol. 1, p. 7-1.
[15] Based on interviews with Jim Dochstader, Sarnia office, Ministry of the Environment, (April 1982), Rick Hunter and Steen Klint, Tricil Limited, Sarnia (December 1981 and July 1982).
[16] Telephone interview with Steen Klint, July 1982.
[17] "Harwich releases report on dumping," *Windsor Star*, 11 March 1981.
[18] Documents released by Township, March 1981.
[19] Authors' interview with Lillian Tomen, June 1980.
[20] Documents released by Township, March 1981.
[21] Legislature of Ontario, *Legislative Debates*, 6 November 1980, p 4175.
[22] Legislature of Ontario, *Legislative Debates*, 3 November 1980, p. 3990.
[23] Letter from D.A. McTavish, Regional Director, Ministry of the Environment to W.M. Phipps, Clerk-Treasurer, Township of Harwich, 28 October 1980.
[24] Keith Norton, Minister of the Environment, Legislature of Ontario, *Legislative Debates*, 16 June 1981, p. 1650.
[25] John Swaigen, *Submission to the Ombudsman on Behalf of the Preserve Our Water Resources Group*, [undated], p. 6.
[26] Authors' interview, November 1981.
[27] *Ibid.*
[28] Letter to Hedy Gervais, Upper Ottawa Street Residents' Association, 17 June 1982.
[29] Authors' interview, July 1980.
[30] Colin Macfarlane, quoted by Gord McNulty, "Smith seeks records of waste firm," *Spectator* [Hamilton], 3 November 1978.
[31] "Merling queries dumping answers," *Spectator*, 28 February 1978.
[32] "Smith seeks records of waste firm," *Spectator*, 3 November 1978.

[33] "Official admits knowing about waste dumping," *Spectator*, 6 March 1979.
[34] "People angry despite dump safety pledge," *Spectator*, 28 October 1980.
[35] Legislature of Ontario, *Legislative Debates*, 20 March 1979.
[36] "I saw PCBs, cyanide go to Ottawa dump," *Spectator*, 6 October 1980.
[37] Legislature of Ontario, *Legislative Debates*, 20 March 1979.
[38] Colin West, quoted in "Region, province disagree on waste testing methods," *Spectator*, 30 July 1979.
[39] Ian Cunningham, quoted in "Dump is poison, woman in Hamilton warns," *Globe and Mail*, 21 December 1979.
[40] Dennis Timbrell, quoted in "Chemical wastes at dump site frighten Hamilton neighbors," *Globe and Mail*, 2 September 1980.
[41] Authors' interview, November 1981.
[42] Paul Isles, quoted by Hon. S.H.S. Hughes, *Report of the Royal Commission Appointed to Inquire into Waste Management Inc., et cetera*, p. 44.
[43] Authors' interview with Mac Graham, December 1981.
[44] D.A. McTavish, *Control Order to Tricil Limited*, 13 January 1978.
[45] Authors' interview, December 1981.
[46] *Op. cit.*, pp 100-101.
[47] "Cleanup breathes life into Elmira creek," *Kitchener-Waterloo Record*, 9 August 1980.
[48] Moni Campbell, "Making Industrial Waste Reduction and Recycling A Viable Alternative to Land Disposal," Brief to Toxic Chemicals Management Centre, Environment Canada, March 1982, p. 2.
[49] "Hazardous Waste Law in Canada," *Canadian Environmental Law Review*, December 1980, p. 158.
[50] Colin Macfarlane, from minutes at meeting, 11 August 1982.
[51] *First Biennial Report under the Great Lakes Water Quality Agreement of 1978*, June 1982, p. 6.
[52] "Must accept some toxic risks: Roberts," *Globe and Mail*, 14 October 1982.
[53] *1981 Report on Great Lakes Water Quality*, November 1981, p. 8.
[54] "Name your poison," 26 May 1980.
[55] Authors' interview, December 1981.
[56] *Ibid.*
[57] Authors' interview, November 1981.
[58] "Uniroyal burden: Bearing high cost of pollution," *Kitchener-Waterloo Record*, 9 August 1980.
[59] Authors' interview with Margherita Howe, December 1981.
[60] Authors' interview with Fran Sutton, June 1982.
[61] Charles Parker, interviewed on CFGM, Richmond Hill, September 1981.
[62] Legislature of Ontario, *Legislative Debates*, 11 June 1981, p. 1486, and 16 June 1981, p. 1650.
[63] Authors' interview, November 1981.
[64] Authors' interview, June 1982.
[65] Legislature of Ontario, *Legislative Debates*, 11 March 1982, p. 31.
[66] Letter from Gerard C. Ronan, Director, Laboratory Services Branch to Dr. J. Cummins, 2 March 1982.
[67] "Norton criticized Star's coverage," *Toronto Star*, 30 April 1982.
[68] "Stouffville test not faked, Norton says," *Toronto Star*, 10 March 1982.

[69] *Ibid.*
[70] Letter from G. Crawford, 21 January 1982.
[71] Authors' interview, June 1982.
[72] Authors' interview, June 1982.
[73] Elva Monroe, quoted by Fran Sutton, *ibid.*
[74] Authors' interview, June 1982.
[75] Ontario Ministry of the Environment, "Whitchurch-Stouffville Chemical Testing Program, Interim Report," May 1982, p. 36.
[76] Authors' interview, June 1982.

Chapter 4: The Search for New Waste Disposal Facilities

[1] Ontario Ministry of the Environment, "Facts," [undated].
[2] See *Environmental Assessment for Solidification Facilities in Harwich Township and in the City of Niagara Falls,* 1980, pp. 3-10 to 3-14.
[3] Ontario Ministry of the Environment, "Facts," August 1980.
[4] "Parrott promulgates industrial waste program," *Ecolog Week,* 27 October 1978.
[5] Ontario Ministry of the Environment, "Facts," [undated].
[6] James F. MacLaren Limited, *Interim Summary Report to the Ministry of the Environment for Development of Treatment and/or Disposal Sites for Liquid Industrial Wastes and Hazardous Wastes,* August 1979.
[7] From notes taken by one of the authors at the meeting, December 1980.
[8] *Ibid.*
[9] Authors' interview, November 1981.
[10] Quoted from "Press Conference Remarks by Dr. D.A. Chant Regarding the Proposed South Cayuga Site for a Secure Landfill," 18 November 1981, p. 7.
[11] Ontario Public Interest Research Group (Hamilton), *The South Cayuga Saga,* October 1981, p. 11.
[12] Ontario Ministry of the Environment, "Facts," August 1980.
[13] Interviews with Lillian Tomen, Diane Jacobs and Greta Thompson, July 1980.
[14] (New York: Cardinal Pocketbooks), pp. 5 & 144.
[15] "Environment officials junk big waste disposal system proposed for Nanticoke," *Globe and Mail,* 24 May 1978.
[16] "Hazardous Waste Siting Requirements: What Role Should be Assumed by Intervenors," *Proceedings of Hazardous Waste Management Seminar,* 26 & 27 October 1978, p. 21-9.
[17] Stephen Garrod, "Environmental Hearings under Ontario's *Environmental Protection Act:* A Case Study in Political Interference," *The CELA Newsletter,* February 1981, p. 6.
[18] Janet Ecker, quoted in "Harwich waste plant on hold," *Windsor Star,* 30 November 1980.
[19] "Hazardous Waste Siting Requirements," p. 21-2.
[20] "The Nimby Syndrome — Another View," [unpublished, 1982], p. 4.
[21] International Joint Commission, *Report on Hazardous Waste Disposal,* July 1978, p. 11.
[22] *Ibid.,* p. 13.
[23] "Final Report," 1979, pp. III & V.

Chapter 5: The Decision-making Process

[1] "Ontario picks Cayuga farmland for industrial waste dump," *Globe and Mail*, 26 November 1980.

[2] From notes taken by author at the meeting, December 1980.

[3] Authors' interview, December 1981.

[4] Fran Sutton, in authors' interview, June 1982.

[5] Authors' interview, November 1981.

[6] Stephen Garrod, "Environmental Hearings under Ontario's *Environmental Protection Act*," *op. cit.*, p. 7.

[7] George Hicks, quoted in Environmental Assessment Board, "Report on the Public Hearing on the Application by the Regional Municipality of Hamilton-Wentworth for Approval of a Waste Disposal Site for Landfilling in the Township of Glanbrook," October 18, 1979, pp. 234-5.

[8] *Report of the Royal Commission, op.cit.*, p. 14.

[9] *Submission to the Ombudsman on Behalf of the Preserve our Water Resources Group*, [undated], p. 21.

[10] "Liquid waste permitted at eight uncertified sites," *Windsor Star*, 2 December 1981.

[11] "Ontario searches for new solutions on industrial waste," *Globe and Mail*, 22 February 1982.

[12] News Release, 9 February 1982.

[13] *Ibid.*

[14] Minutes taken at meeting, 11 August 1982.

[15] *Ontario Waste Management Corporation Act*, 1981, Sec. 15 (2).

[16] Legislature of Ontario, *Legislative Debates*, 25 November 1980, p. 4595.

Chapter 6: Towards a New Waste Management System

[1] Council on Environmental Quality, U.S. Department of State, *Global Future: Time to Act*, January 1981, p. xiii.

[2] California Office of Appropriate Technology, *Alternatives to Land Disposal of Hazardous Wastes*, 1981, p. 92.

[3] Monica E. Campbell and William M. Glenn, *Profit from Pollution Prevention* (Toronto: Pollution Probe Foundation, 1982), p. 2.

[4] *Hazardous Waste Reduction and Reclamation*, March 1981, p. ii.

[5] *Ibid.*, p. 7.

[6] *Op. cit.*, p. 105.

[7] Katherine A. Durso-Hughes, "Once is not enough," *Exposure*, May 1981, p. 3.

[8] *Ibid.*, p. 6.

[9] *Ibid.*

[10] *Op. cit.*, p. 163.

[11] Moni Campbell, "Making Industrial Waste Reduction and Recycling a Viable Alternative to Land Disposal," Brief to the Toxic Chemicals Management Centre, Environment Canada, March 1982, p. 2.

[12] The description of these technologies is based primarily upon California Office of Appropriate Technology, *op. cit.*, and Environment Council of Alberta, *Hazardous Waste Management in Alberta: Report and Recommendations*, December 1980.

[13] *Op. cit.,* p. 230.
[14] "What to do with hazardous wastes," November/December 1981, p. 43.
[15] "Answering the critics," December 1980, p. 18.
[16] *Op. cit.,* p. 219.
[17] "Incineration may be best disposal method for most hazardous wastes," *Solid Waste Management,* April 1980, p. 122.
[18] *Federal Register,* Vol. 46, no. 24, 5 February 1981.
[19] Pollution Probe, *Hazardous Waste Reduction and Reclamation,* p. 11 and Campbell and Glenn, *op. cit.,* p. 133.
[20] Cited in Janice Crossland, "The Wastes Endure," *Environment,* June/July 1977, p. 11.
[21] Kurt Riegel, cited in Katherine Durso-Hughes and James Lewis, "Recycling Hazardous Wastes," *Environment,* March 1982, p. 14.

Chapter 7: Conclusion
[1] From notes taken at HOPE meeting, November 1981.
[2] Interview on CBET television, Windsor, November 1980.

Appendix: Hazardous Wastes across Canada
[1] Gore & Storrie, *Canadian National Inventory of Hazardous Wastes* (Environment Canada, January 1982), 3 vols.
[2] *A Summary Report on Hazardous Wastes, Maritime Provinces,* p. 3.
[3] Ian Travers, quoted by David Ogilvie, "Canada: Weak Controls from Sea to Shining Sea," *Ambio,* 1982.
[4] *Assessment of Maritime Hazardous Waste Inventory Report as it Applies to Nova Scotia.*
[5] *A Summary Report on Hazardous Wastes, Maritime Provinces,* p. 3.
[6] Ian Travers, *op. cit.*
[7] "Disposal of waste mishandled: N.B. study," *Globe and Mail,* 27 April 1982.
[8] *Ibid.*
[9] "Quebeckers upset over toxic waste plant on 'unsuitable' land," *Globe and Mail,* 22 July 1981.
[10] "Three companies charged for dumping illegal waste," *Gazette,* 2 October 1982.
[11] Ontario Waste Management Corporation, *Waste Quantities Study,* p. 58.
[12] *Development of a Waste Management Plan,* vol. 3 of *Hazardous Waste in Northern & Western Canada,* (Environment Canada, undated).
[13] Reid, Crowther & Partners Ltd., *Hazardous Waste in Northern & Western Canada,* vol. 1, p. 162.
[14] *Ibid.,* pp. 160-3.
[15] *Ibid.,* p. 158.
[16] Ian Travers, *op. cit.*
[17] Environment Council of Alberta, *Hazardous Waste Management in Alberta,* p.24.
[18] "Worry over waste," *Globe and Mail,* 28 June 1980.
[19] "Where can waste go if nobody wants it?", *Globe and Mail,* 9 July 1981.
[20] Reid, Crowther & Partners Ltd., *op. cit.,* vol. 1, p. 120.
[21] Bob Sass and Richard Butler, "The poisoning of Canada," *Canadian Dimension,* May 1982, p. 6.

INDEX